CONTENTS

THE RIGHT SIZE

This handy guide to average serving sizes will help those who are unsure about how much to cook or buy. Active people may find that they need slightly larger helpings of foods such as pasta, rice and potatoes.

Frozen beans
60 g/2 oz

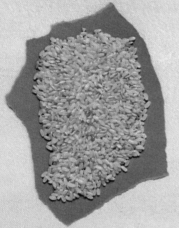

Frozen peas
60 g/2 oz

Brown rice
45 g/1¹/2 oz

Canned corn kernels
100 g/3¹/2 oz

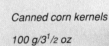

White rice
45 g/1¹/2 oz

Steak
125 g/4 oz

Boneless chicken breast fille

125 g/4 oz

COOKING FOR ONE

UK COOKERY EDITOR
Katie Swallow

EDITORIAL
Food Editor: Rachel Blackmore
Assistant Food Editor: Anneka Mitchell
Home Economist: Donna Hay
Editorial Coordinator: Margaret Kelly
Subeditor: Ella Martin

PHOTOGRAPHY
Andy Payne

STYLING
Anneka Mitchell, Donna Hay

DESIGN AND PRODUCTION
Manager: Sheridan Carter
Layout: Lulu Dougherty
Finished Art: Stephen Joseph
Cover Design: Frank Pithers

Includes Index
ISBN 1 85391 249 2
ISBN 1 86343 031 8 (pbk)

Published by J.B. Fairfax Press Pty Ltd
80-82 McLachlan Avenue
Rushcutters Bay NSW 2011
Australia

Formatted by J.B. Fairfax Press Pty Ltd
Output by Adtype, Sydney
Printed by Toppan Printing Co.
Hong Kong

Distributed by J.B. Fairfax Press Pty Ltd
9 Trinity Centre, Park Farm Estate
Wellingborough, Northants
Ph: (0933) 402330   Fax: (0933) 402234

*T*his book is especially for those people who eat alone, either regularly or occasionally, and want to eat wholesome, home-cooked meals. Remember that the keys to a healthy lifestyle are a balanced diet and exercise. When you cook you can choose what you want to eat and you are able to ensure that the freshest possible ingredients are used – good reasons for taking the time to prepare your own food. Whether it's a main meal, snack, dessert or cake you are looking for, this book gives you a variety of recipes to suit your mood and the occasion. Filled with useful hints and tips on adapting recipes, what to do with leftovers, shopping for one, cook-ahead meals, freezing information – and much more – **Cooking for One** is the perfect companion for any single cook.

THE PANTRY SHELF

Unless otherwise stated, the following ingredients used in this book are:

Cream   Double, suitable for whipping
Flour   White flour, plain or standard
Sugar   White sugar

WHAT'S IN A TABLESPOON?

AUSTRALIA
1 tablespoon   20 mL   4 teaspoons

NEW ZEALAND
1 tablespoon   15 mL   3 teaspoons

UNITED KINGDOM
1 tablespoon   15 mL   3 teaspoons

The recipes in this book were tested in Australia where a 20 mL tablespoon is standard. All measures are level.

The tablespoon in the New Zealand and United Kingdom set of measuring spoons is 15 mL. In many recipes this difference will not matter. For recipes using baking powder, gelatine, bicarbonate of soda, or small quantities of flour and cornflour, simply add another teaspoon for each tablespoon specified.

CANNED FOODS

Can sizes vary between countries and manufacturers. You may find the quantities in this book are slightly different from what is available. Purchase and use the can size nearest to the suggested size in the recipe.

Fresh pasta

First course: 75-100 g/2$\frac{1}{2}$-3$\frac{1}{2}$ oz

Main meal: 100-155 g/3$\frac{1}{2}$-5 oz

Dried pasta

First course: 60-75 g/2-2$\frac{1}{2}$ oz

Main meal: 75-100 g/2$\frac{1}{2}$-3$\frac{1}{2}$ oz

Canned fruit
(such as peaches, pears,
apricots, apples)

100 g/3$\frac{1}{2}$ oz

Filled pasta

First course: 155-185 g/5-6 oz

Main meal: 185-200 g/6-6$\frac{1}{2}$ oz

Potatoes
90 g/3 oz

Lamb chops

155-185 g/5-6 oz

Fish

100 g/3$\frac{1}{2}$ oz

Rectangle dish and oval dishes The Bay Tree *Plates* Accoutrement

MAIN MEALS

This selection of delicious main course dishes shows how easy it is to cook for one and how enjoyable eating alone can be.

Rack of Lamb with Rosemary, Lamb Curry (recipes page 8)

Fabric, pillow and napkin Les Olivades Blue-rimmed plate Royal Doulton Open dish Waterford Wedgwood Table Corso De Fiori

RACK OF LAMB WITH ROSEMARY

You might like to use other vegetables, such as zucchini (courgettes), onions and parsnip in this recipe.

Makes 2 servings
Oven temperature 180°C, 350°F, Gas 4

- ☐ **1 potato, peeled and halved**
- ☐ **2 tablespoons olive oil**
- ☐ **1 piece pumpkin, peeled**
- ☐ **1 carrot, peeled and halved lengthwise**
- ☐ **1 rack of lamb with 6 cutlets**
- ☐ **6 small sprigs fresh rosemary**
- ☐ **1 clove garlic, thinly sliced**

1   Bring a saucepan of water, to the boil, add potato and boil for 4-5 minutes. Drain and dry on absorbent kitchen paper. Place oil in a baking dish and heat in oven for 5 minutes. Add potato, pumpkin and carrot, and cook for 20 minutes, turning and basting occasionally with oil.

2   Make six small slits in meat and place a sprig of rosemary and a sliver of garlic in each slit. Add rack of lamb to baking dish and cook for 30-35 minutes or until vegetables are tender and meat is cooked to your liking.

Serving suggestion: Cut lamb into a rack of 3 cutlets and serve with roast vegetables and a green vegetable such as broccoli or beans.

Leftovers tip: Team leftover lamb with chutney or relish to make a delicious sandwich for lunch the next day. Or use it to make a tasty curry for dinner the next night. To make lamb curry, crush $^1/_2$ clove garlic and chop $^1/_2$ onion. Heat 2 teaspoons oil in a nonstick frying pan and cook garlic and onion over a medium heat for 3-4 minutes or until onion softens. Add 1 teaspoon curry powder, $^1/_2$ teaspoon garam masala, $^1/_4$ teaspoon ground cloves and a pinch of ginger and cook for 1 minute longer. Stir in $^1/_3$ cup/90 mL/3 fl oz beef stock, bring to simmering and simmer for 10-15 minutes or until mixture reduces and thickens slightly. Cut leftover cooked lamb into 1 cm/$^1/_2$ in cubes. Add lamb to frying pan and cook for 4-5 minutes or until heated through. Just prior to serving, stir in 1$^1/_2$ tablespoons natural yogurt. Sprinkle with 2 teaspoons toasted slivered almonds and serve immediately.

Plate Waterford Wedgwood *Chair Corso De Fiori*

SEAFOOD SOUP

Makes 2 servings

- ☐ **4 mussels, scrubbed and beards removed**
- ☐ **$^1/_3$ cup/90 mL/3 fl oz dry white wine**
- ☐ **2 teaspoons olive oil**
- ☐ **1 clove garlic, crushed**
- ☐ **pinch chilli powder**
- ☐ **1 small leek, finely sliced**
- ☐ **2 tomatoes, peeled, seeded and chopped**
- ☐ **3 cups/750 mL/1$^1/_4$ pt chicken stock**
- ☐ **1 tablespoon tomato paste (purée)**
- ☐ **30 g/1 oz rice noodles**
- ☐ **1 spinach leaf, finely shredded**
- ☐ **30 g/1 oz bean sprouts**
- ☐ **8 uncooked prawns, peeled and deveined**
- ☐ **1 tablespoon chopped fresh coriander or parsley**
- ☐ **1 tablespoon grated fresh Parmesan cheese**

1   Place mussels and wine in a frying pan, cover and cook over a high heat until mussels open. Discard any mussels that do not open after 5 minutes. Remove mussels from pan using a slotted spoon.

2   Heat oil in a saucepan and cook garlic, chilli powder and leek over a medium heat for 2-3 minutes or until leek softens. Add tomatoes, stock and tomato paste (purée), cover, bring to simmering and simmer for 15-20 minutes.

STIR-FRY PORK

This stir-fry is just as delicious made with rump steak instead of pork.

Makes 1 serving

- ☐ **30 g/1 oz vermicelli noodles**
- ☐ **1 tablespoon polyunsaturated oil**
- ☐ **125 g/4 oz lean pork, cut into strips**
- ☐ **1 clove garlic, crushed**
- ☐ **¹/₂ teaspoon grated fresh ginger**
- ☐ **1 small onion, cut into eighths**
- ☐ **1 small carrot, cut into thin strips**
- ☐ **1 small zucchini (courgette), cut into thin strips**
- ☐ **45 g/1¹/₂ oz snow peas (mangetout), trimmed**
- ☐ **1 teaspoon cornflour blended with 2 tablespoons beef stock**
- ☐ **1 tablespoon soy sauce**
- ☐ **1 tablespoon dry sherry**

1   Cook noodles in boiling water in a saucepan following packet directions. Drain, set aside and keep warm.

2   Heat 2 teaspoons oil in a nonstick frying pan or wok and stir-fry pork in batches over a high heat until it just changes colour. Remove pork from pan and drain on absorbent kitchen paper.

3   Heat remaining oil in pan, add garlic, ginger, onion, carrot and zucchini (courgette) and stir-fry for 2-3 minutes. Stir in snow peas (mangetout) and cook for 2 minutes longer.

4   Combine cornflour mixture, soy sauce and sherry. Return pork to pan and add noodles and cornflour mixture. Cook, stirring, for 2-3 minutes or until mixture thickens and meat is heated through.

Left: Stir-fry Pork
Below: Seafood Soup

3   Add noodles and cook for 2 minutes. Stir in spinach, bean sprouts, prawns, mussels and coriander or parsley, and cook for 1-2 minutes longer or until prawns change colour.

Serving suggestion: Sprinkle with grated fresh Parmesan cheese and accompany with thick toast.

Freeze it: This soup can be frozen before adding the seafood. Defrost soup in refrigerator overnight and reheat in a saucepan over a medium heat. The soup can also be reheated from frozen. Place frozen soup in a saucepan and heat gently until soup is liquid. Bring to the boil, then add seafood and cook until prawns change colour.

Plate and butter dish Accoutrement

Plates Waterford Wedgwood Napkin Les Olivades

BAKED SPICY FILLET

Makes 1 serving
Oven temperature 200°C, 400°F, Gas 6

- ☐ **1 tablespoon lemon juice**
- ☐ **2 teaspoons soy sauce**
- ☐ **pinch curry powder**
- ☐ **pinch mustard powder**
- ☐ **freshly ground black pepper**
- ☐ **1 x 125-155 g/4-5 oz firm white fish fillet, such as perch, whiting or ling**
- ☐ **15 g/^{1}/$_2$ oz butter**

1　Combine lemon juice, soy sauce, curry powder, mustard powder and black pepper to taste in a bowl.

2　Brush fish fillet with lemon juice mixture and place in a greased baking dish. Dot with butter and bake for 15 minutes or until fish flakes when tested with a fork.

Serving suggestion: A crisp salad and boiled new potatoes will complete this meal.

FISH ROLL WITH SPINACH AND LEMON SAUCE

Makes 1 serving
Oven temperature 180°C, 350°F, Gas 4

- ☐ **15 g/^{1}/$_2$ oz butter**
- ☐ **^{1}/$_2$ clove garlic, crushed**
- ☐ **1 teaspoon pine nuts**
- ☐ **1 spinach leaf, shredded**
- ☐ **pinch ground nutmeg**
- ☐ **1 tablespoon grated tasty cheese (mature Cheddar)**
- ☐ **freshly ground black pepper**
- ☐ **1 x 125-155 g/4-5 oz white fish fillet, such as perch, whiting or ling**

LEMON SAUCE
- ☐ **15 g/^{1}/$_2$ oz butter**
- ☐ **2 teaspoons flour**
- ☐ **^{1}/$_4$ cup/60 mL/2 fl oz chicken stock**
- ☐ **^{1}/$_4$ cup/60 mL/2 fl oz milk**
- ☐ **1 teaspoon lemon juice**
- ☐ **freshly ground black pepper**

1　Melt butter in a frying pan and cook garlic and pine nuts over a medium heat for 2-3 minutes or until nuts are golden. Add spinach and cook until wilted. Remove from heat and stir in nutmeg and cheese. Season to taste with black pepper and set aside to cool.

2　Place spinach mixture down centre of fish fillet, roll up and secure with wooden cocktail sticks or toothpicks. Place in a greased baking dish and bake for 15-20 minutes or until fish flakes when tested with a fork.

3　To make sauce, melt butter in a small saucepan, stir in flour and cook over a medium heat for 1 minute. Remove pan from heat and gradually mix in stock and milk. Cook over a medium heat, stirring constantly, until mixture boils and thickens. Stir in lemon juice and season to taste with black pepper. Serve with fish roll.

Serving suggestion: Accompany with boiled, steamed or microwaved asparagus and carrot, and sautéed mushrooms.

MARINATED PEPPER STEAK

Makes 1 serving

- ☐ **2 tablespoons olive oil**
- ☐ **2 teaspoons lemon juice**
- ☐ **2 teaspoons cracked black pepper**
- ☐ **1 clove garlic, crushed**
- ☐ **1 boneless rib-eye or fillet steak**

1 Place oil, lemon juice, black pepper and garlic in a shallow glass or ceramic dish. Mix to combine. Add steak and set aside to marinate for as long as possible. Turn once or twice during marinating.

2 Remove steak from marinade and reserve marinade. Cook steak under a preheated medium-high grill for 3-4 minutes each side, or until cooked to your liking. Brush frequently with reserved marinade during cooking.

Serving suggestion: Accompany with boiled, steamed or microwaved carrot, zucchini ribbons and brown rice.

Easy marinating: An easy way of marinating one steak is to place the steak and marinade in a plastic food bag, tie securely and set aside to marinate, turning the bag several times. If you plan ahead and marinate your steak overnight, this will allow the flavour to develop.

Beef Kebabs: Try cutting the steak into 2 cm/^{3}/$_4$ in cubes, before marinating and threading onto lightly oiled wooden skewers. Then grill or barbecue for delicious kebabs.

Left: Baked Spicy Fillet, Fish Roll with Spinach and Lemon Sauce
Below: Marinated Pepper Steak, Beef Kebabs

Plates, glass and salt and pepper shakers Waterford Wedgwood Cutlery Bay Tree

HAMBURGER

Makes 1 serving

- [ ] 1 teaspoon oil
- [ ] 1 sesame hamburger bun or roll, split, toasted and buttered
- [ ] 1 tablespoon grated tasty cheese (mature Cheddar)
- [ ] 1 slice cooked beetroot
- [ ] 1 slice tomato
- [ ] 1 lettuce leaf

MEAT PATTIE
- [ ] 100 g/3^1/2 oz beef mince
- [ ] 2 tablespoons bread crumbs, made from stale bread
- [ ] 1 tablespoon chopped onion
- [ ] 1 teaspoon soy sauce
- [ ] 2 teaspoons tomato sauce
- [ ] ^{1}/4 teaspoon dried mixed herbs
- [ ] 1 egg yolk
- [ ] freshly ground black pepper

1 To make pattie, place beef, bread crumbs, onion, soy sauce, tomato sauce, mixed herbs and egg yolk in a bowl and mix to combine. Season to taste with black pepper.

2 Shape meat mixture into a pattie using wet hands. Heat oil in a nonstick frying pan and cook pattie over a medium-high heat for 4-5 minutes each side or until cooked to your liking.

3 To assemble hamburger, sprinkle bottom half of bun with cheese, and then top with pattie, beetroot, tomato, lettuce and top half of bun.

Freeze it: This hamburger pattie freezes well. You can multiply the pattie recipe to make as many as you wish. Freeze the patties individually in airtight freezerproof containers or sealed freezer bags. Patties can be frozen before or after cooking. Defrost patties overnight in the refrigerator, or in the microwave for 1-2 minutes on DEFROST (30%). Cook or reheat in a nonstick frying pan or on the hotplate (griddle) of a barbecue.

Cook's tip: Variations for hamburgers are endless. Try adding finely grated vegetables – such as carrot or zucchini – to the pattie mixture, or other sauces, such as Worcestershire sauce. You may like to place the pattie in a pitta bread. Using a fork, break up the cooked pattie and spread over bread, then top with your choice of ingredients and roll up. Vary the flavour by using different mustards, relishes, chutneys, sauces and vegetables.

Pink Juperana Marble Marble and Granite Art Glass Home & Garden

Hamburger

QUICK TASTY CHICKEN

Allowing the chicken to marinate overnight will give this tasty dish even more flavour.

Makes 1 serving

- [ ] 1^1/2 tablespoons soy sauce
- [ ] 3 teaspoons honey, warmed
- [ ] 2 teaspoons dry sherry
- [ ] 2 teaspoons lemon juice
- [ ] 2 teaspoons sesame oil
- [ ] 1 clove garlic, crushed
- [ ] ^{1}/2 teaspoon grated fresh ginger
- [ ] 1 boneless chicken breast fillet

1 Combine soy sauce, honey, sherry, lemon juice, oil, garlic and ginger in a shallow glass or ceramic dish. Add chicken breast, cover and set aside to marinate for 30 minutes or overnight in the refrigerator.

2 Remove chicken from marinade and cook under a preheated medium grill, brushing with marinade, for 4-5 minutes each side or until cooked.

Serving suggestion: Serve with boiled noodles tossed with freshly ground black pepper and boiled, steamed or microwaved sugar snap peas.

Cook's tip: Cooked chicken dishes that are to be frozen should be cooled quickly and completely before freezing. To quickly cool a cooked chicken dish, place saucepan in a sink of iced water and stir from time to time or until cooled. Remember, if you have cooked in ovenproof glass or ceramic dishes, you will need to transfer the cooked mixture to another container, or the sudden change in temperature may cause the dish to break. Uncooked chicken should be prepared in the form you wish to use it before freezing.

FETTUCCINE WITH CREAMY CHICKEN

Makes 1 serving

- [ ] 75 g/2$^{1}/_{2}$ oz fettuccine
- [ ] 30 g/1 oz butter
- [ ] 1 boneless chicken breast fillet, cut into strips
- [ ] 1 clove garlic, crushed
- [ ] 45 g/1$^{1}/_{2}$ oz button mushrooms, sliced
- [ ] 1 slice ham, chopped
- [ ] $^{1}/_{3}$ cup/90 mL/3 fl oz cream (double)
- [ ] 2 teaspoons chopped fresh basil
- [ ] freshly ground black pepper

1 Cook fettuccine in boiling water in a saucepan following packet directions. Drain, set aside and keep warm.

2 Melt 15 g/$^{1}/_{2}$ oz butter in a nonstick frying pan and cook chicken strips over a medium-high heat for 2-3 minutes or until just cooked. Remove from pan and drain on absorbent kitchen paper.

3 Melt remaining butter in pan and cook garlic and mushrooms over a high heat for 1-2 minutes. Add ham and cream, reduce heat and simmer for 2-3 minutes or until sauce thickens. Return chicken to pan, stir in basil and cook until heated. Season to taste with black pepper. Spoon sauce over fettuccine to serve.

Serving suggestion: Accompany with boiled, steamed or microwaved broccoli, carrots and snow peas (mangetout).

Quick Tasty Chicken, Fettuccine with Creamy Chicken

Plates and glass Waterford Wedgwood

13

Plates Waterford Wedgwood

PASTA WITH CRAB

In this recipe, fresh pasta can be used instead of dried pasta and will take only 3-4 minutes to cook.

Makes 1 serving

- ☐ **75 g /2¹/₂ oz tomato tagliatelle or fettuccine**
- ☐ **15 g/¹/₂ oz butter**
- ☐ **1 clove garlic, crushed**
- ☐ **1 small leek, finely sliced**
- ☐ **1 zucchini (courgette), cut into thin strips**

- ☐ **90 g/3 oz fresh crab meat, chopped, or canned crab meat, drained**
- ☐ **1 teaspoon lime juice**
- ☐ **freshly ground black pepper**
- ☐ **1 tablespoon sour cream**

1 Cook tagliatelle or fettuccine in boiling water in a saucepan following packet directions. Drain, set aside and keep warm.

2 Melt butter in a nonstick frying pan and cook garlic and leek over a medium heat for 3-4 minutes or until leek softens. Add zucchini (courgette) and cook for 2 minutes

longer. Add tagliatelle or fettuccine, crab meat and lime juice, and season to taste with black pepper. Cook for 3-4 minutes or until heated. Remove from heat, stir in sour cream and serve immediately.

Serving suggestion: Sprinkle with grated Parmesan cheese and accompany with crusty bread.

Fish with Julienne Vegetables, Pasta with Crab

FISH WITH JULIENNE VEGETABLES

Makes 1 serving

- ☐ 1 tablespoon oil
- ☐ 185 g/6 oz firm white fish fillet, such as perch, whiting or ling, cut into cubes
- ☐ 1 small carrot, cut into thin strips
- ☐ 2 spring onions, cut into thin strips
- ☐ 1/2 red pepper, cut into thin strips
- ☐ 1/2 teaspoon grated fresh ginger
- ☐ 1 teaspoon cornflour blended with 2 tablespoons water
- ☐ 1 teaspoon dry sherry
- ☐ 2 teaspoons soy sauce
- ☐ freshly ground black pepper

1   Heat 2 teaspoons oil in a frying pan and cook fish over a high heat for 2-3 minutes or until just cooked. Remove from pan and set aside.

2   Heat remaining oil in frying pan and cook carrot, spring onions, red pepper and ginger over a medium-high heat for 2-3 minutes. Combine cornflour mixture, sherry and soy sauce. Return fish to pan, stir in cornflour mixture and cook, stirring constantly, for 2-3 minutes longer or until heated. Season to taste with black pepper.

Serving suggestion: Spoon fish mixture over boiled egg noodles and sprinkle with finely chopped coriander or parsley.

CHICKEN SALAD WITH ORANGE DRESSING

This salad is also delicious if you use barbecued chicken.

Makes 1 serving

- ☐ 2 teaspoons olive oil
- ☐ 1 boneless chicken breast fillet, cut into strips
- ☐ 3 lettuce leaves, torn into pieces
- ☐ 1 small carrot, cut into thin strips
- ☐ 1 small tomato, cut into wedges
- ☐ 4 stalks asparagus, blanched and cut into 5 cm/2 in lengths, or 4 stalks canned asparagus
- ☐ 1 tablespoon pine nuts, toasted
- ☐ 2 teaspoons snipped fresh chives

ORANGE DRESSING
- ☐ 1/4 cup/45 g/1 1/2 oz natural yogurt
- ☐ 3 teaspoons orange juice
- ☐ 1/2 teaspoon finely grated orange rind

1   Heat oil in a nonstick frying pan and cook chicken strips over a medium-high heat for 2-3 minutes or until cooked. Remove chicken from pan and set aside to cool on absorbent kitchen paper.

2   To make dressing, place yogurt, orange juice and orange rind in a bowl and whisk to combine.

3   Arrange lettuce, carrot, tomato, asparagus and chicken attractively on a serving plate. Sprinkle with pine nuts and chives, then spoon over dressing.

Plate Villeroy & Boch

Chicken Salad with Orange Dressing

DRESSINGS

Dressings add interest to any salad or vegetable. All of these dressings are quick to make and can be kept in the refrigerator for a week or more.

MAYONNAISE

Makes 1^1/2 cups/375 mL/12 fl oz

- ☐ 2 egg yolks
- ☐ ^{1}/4 teaspoon mustard powder
- ☐ 1 cup/250 mL/8 fl oz olive oil
- ☐ 2 tablespoons lemon juice or white wine vinegar
- ☐ freshly ground black pepper

Place egg yolks and mustard powder in a food processor or blender and process until just combined. With machine running, gradually pour in olive oil and process until mixture thickens. Blend in lemon juice or vinegar and season with black pepper.

Green Herbed Mayonnaise: Purée 30 g/ 1 oz basil leaves, 2 tablespoons chopped fresh parsley, 12 chives and 1 clove garlic. Prepare mayonnaise as above using vinegar in place of lemon juice. Mix basil mixture into mayonnaise.

Blue Cheese Mayonnaise: Crumble 90 g/3 oz blue cheese and blend into prepared mayonnaise.

Storage: Place mayonnaise in a screwtop jar and store in the refrigerator for up to 1 week.

LOW-OIL VINAIGRETTE

Makes 1 cup/250 mL/8 fl oz

- ☐ ^{1}/3 cup/90 mL/3 fl oz olive oil
- ☐ ^{2}/3 cup/170 mL/5^1/2 fl oz cider vinegar
- ☐ ^{1}/2 teaspoon mustard powder
- ☐ cayenne pepper
- ☐ freshly ground black pepper

Place oil, vinegar and mustard in a screwtop jar. Season to taste with cayenne and black pepper and shake well to combine.

Storage: Store vinaigrette in the refrigerator for 2-3 weeks, in the jar in which you made it.

ORIENTAL MAYONNAISE

A delicious sauce to serve with hot vegetables.

Makes 1^1/2 cups/375 mL/12 fl oz

- ☐ 1 clove garlic, crushed
- ☐ 2 teaspoons grated fresh ginger
- ☐ ^{1}/3 cup/90 mL/3 fl oz soy sauce
- ☐ 2 tablespoons cider vinegar
- ☐ 2 tablespoons soft brown sugar
- ☐ 1 teaspoon fennel seeds
- ☐ ^{3}/4 cup/185 mL/6 fl oz vegetable oil
- ☐ 2 teaspoons sesame oil
- ☐ 2 egg yolks
- ☐ ^{1}/2 teaspoon dry mustard
- ☐ ^{1}/2 teaspoon hot chilli sauce

1 Place garlic, ginger, soy sauce, vinegar, sugar and fennel seeds in a small saucepan and bring to the boil. Reduce heat and simmer, uncovered, for 5 minutes or until mixture reduces by half. Remove from heat and strain to remove fennel seeds. Set aside to cool.

2 Combine vegetable and sesame oils. Place egg yolks and mustard powder in a food processor or blender and process until just combined. With machine running, gradually pour in oil mixture. Process until mayonnaise thickens.

3 Add soy mixture and process to combine. Mix in chilli sauce to taste.

Storage: Place mayonnaise in a screwtop jar or bottle and store in the refrigerator for up to 1 week.

GINGER AND SOY DRESSING

This dressing is best made a day before using, to allow the flavours to develop.

Makes 1 cup/250 mL/8 fl oz

- ☐ 1 tablespoon sesame oil
- ☐ 1 tablespoon grated fresh ginger
- ☐ ^{1}/2 cup/125 mL/4 fl oz soy sauce
- ☐ ^{1}/2 cup/125 mL/4 fl oz water
- ☐ 1 tablespoon cider vinegar
- ☐ 1 clove garlic, crushed (optional)

Place oil, ginger, soy sauce, water, vinegar and garlic in a screwtop jar and shake well to combine. Allow to stand at least 15 minutes before using.

Storage: Store dressing in the refrigerator for 2-3 weeks, in the jar in which you made it.

VINAIGRETTE

Makes 1 cup/250 mL/8 fl oz

- ☐ ^{3}/4 cup/185 mL/6 fl oz olive oil
- ☐ ^{1}/4 cup/60 mL/2 fl oz cider vinegar
- ☐ 1 tablespoon Dijon mustard
- ☐ freshly ground black pepper

Place oil, vinegar, and mustard in a screwtop jar. Season to taste with black pepper and shake well to combine.

Walnut or Hazelnut Vinaigrette: Replace olive oil with 3 tablespoons walnut or hazelnut oil and ^{1}/2 cup/125 mL/4 fl oz vegetable oil.

Lemon Herb Vinaigrette: Replace vinegar with 3 tablespoons lemon juice and add 60 g/2 oz mixed chopped herbs such as basil, parsley, chives, rosemary, thyme or tarragon.

Storage: Store Vinaigrette in the refrigerator for 2-3 weeks, in the jar in which you made it.

YOGURT DRESSING

Makes 1 cup/250 mL/8 fl oz

- ☐ ¾ cup/155 g/5 oz natural yogurt
- ☐ 1 clove garlic, crushed (optional)
- ☐ 2 tablespoons white wine vinegar
- ☐ 2 tablespoons snipped fresh chives

Place yogurt, garlic, vinegar and chives in a bowl and whisk to combine.

Mint Yogurt Dressing: Prepare Yogurt Dressing as above. Mix in 2 tablespoons finely chopped fresh mint.

Curried Yogurt Dressing: Prepare Yogurt Dressing as above. Blend in 1 teaspoon curry powder and a dash of chilli sauce.

Thousand Island Yogurt Dressing: Prepare Yogurt Dressing as above, omitting garlic. Mix in 2 tablespoons chopped green olives, 2 finely chopped spring onions, 1 chopped hard-boiled egg, 1 tablespoon finely chopped green pepper, 1 tablespoon tomato paste (purée) and ½ teaspoon chilli sauce.

Storage: Place dressing in a screwtop jar and store in the refrigerator for up to 1 week.

From top: Mayonnaise, Oriental Mayonnaise, Yogurt Dressing, Vinaigrette, Low-oil Vinaigrette, Ginger and Soy Dressing

SALADS

Salads take only minutes to prepare and are delicious eaten as an accompaniment or as a light meal on their own. What could be more wonderful than Garden Salad with Creamy Mayonnaise served with crusty bread and followed by a bowl of soup?

PESTO PASTA SALAD

This salad can be served warm – keep the pasta warm after cooking.

Makes 1 serving

- ☐ **45 g/1¹/₂ oz spiral pasta**
- ☐ **4 cherry tomatoes, halved**
- ☐ **1 slice leg ham, cut into thin strips**
- ☐ **30 g/1 oz watercress or snow pea sprouts**

PESTO SAUCE
- ☐ **15 g/¹/₂ oz fresh basil leaves**
- ☐ **1 clove garlic**
- ☐ **3 teaspoons pine nuts**
- ☐ **2 tablespoons olive oil**
- ☐ **1¹/₂ tablespoons grated fresh Parmesan cheese**
- ☐ **freshly ground black pepper**

1 Cook pasta in a saucepan in boiling water following packet directions. Rinse, drain and set aside to cool.

2 To make sauce, place basil, garlic, pine nuts, and 1 tablespoon oil in a food processor or blender and process until smooth. With machine running, gradually add remaining oil. Mix in Parmesan cheese and season to taste with black pepper.

3 Spoon sauce over pasta and toss to combine. Add tomatoes, ham and watercress or snow pea sprouts to salad and toss.

Cook's tip: This is a wonderful main course salad. To serve as a main course, simply increase the pasta quantity to 60-90 g/2-3 oz.

GARDEN SALAD WITH CREAMY MAYONNAISE

Makes 1 serving

- ☐ **4 lettuce leaves, torn into pieces**
- ☐ **4 cherry tomatoes or tomato wedges**
- ☐ **1 hard-boiled egg, cut into wedges**
- ☐ **4 button mushrooms, sliced**
- ☐ **6 snow peas (mangetout) or sugar snap peas**
- ☐ **1 teaspoon chopped fresh parsley**
- ☐ **1 teaspoon chopped fresh basil**
- ☐ **2 teaspoons pine nuts, toasted**
- ☐ **Croutons (see recipe)**
- ☐ **Mayonnaise (page 16) or Yogurt Dressing (page 17)**

Arrange lettuce, tomatoes, egg, mushrooms and snow peas (mangetout) or sugar snap peas on a serving plate. Sprinkle with parsley, basil, pine nuts and croutons. Spoon over a little Mayonnaise or Yogurt Dressing and serve immediately.

Croutons: To make Croutons, cut crusts from a slice of bread, then lightly brush with oil and cut into cubes. Place cubes on a baking tray and bake at 200°C/400°F/Gas 6 for 10-15 minutes or until Croutons are golden and crisp.

From left: Waldorf Salad, Garden Salad with Creamy Mayonnaise, Pesto Pasta Salad, Julienne Vegetable Salad, Simple Green Salad

SIMPLE GREEN SALAD

Makes 1 serving

- ☐ **4 small lettuce leaves**
- ☐ **6 slices cucumber**
- ☐ **$1/4$ green pepper, cut into thin strips**
- ☐ **1 spring onion, finely chopped**
- ☐ **1 teaspoon snipped fresh chives**
- ☐ **1 teaspoon finely chopped fresh parsley**
- ☐ **freshly ground black pepper**
- ☐ **Vinaigrette (page 16) or Low-oil Vinaigrette (page 16)**

Arrange lettuce, cucumber, green pepper and spring onion on a serving plate. Sprinkle with chives and parsley and season to taste with black pepper. Drizzle with Vinaigrette or Low-oil Vinaigrette.

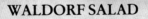

WALDORF SALAD

Makes 1 serving

- ☐ **1 green or red apple, cored and sliced**
- ☐ **1 teaspoon lemon juice**
- ☐ **$1/2$ stalk celery, sliced**
- ☐ **1 tablespoon roughly chopped walnuts**
- ☐ **$1^1/2$ tablespoons Mayonnaise (page 16) or Yogurt Dressing (page 17)**
- ☐ **freshly grated black pepper**

Place apple in a bowl, pour lemon juice over and toss to coat. Add celery, walnuts and Mayonnaise or Yogurt Dressing and toss to combine. Season to taste with black pepper.

JULIENNE VEGETABLE SALAD

Makes 1 serving

- ☐ **1 small carrot, cut into thin strips**
- ☐ **1 small zucchini (courgette), cut into thin strips**
- ☐ **$1/2$ stalk celery, cut into thin strips**
- ☐ **Ginger and Soy Dressing (page 16)**
- ☐ **1 teaspoon sesame seeds, toasted**

Arrange carrot, zucchini (courgette) and celery on a serving plate. Drizzle with Ginger and Soy Dressing and sprinkle with sesame seeds.

Large bowls and spoon The Bay Tree Plates Accoutrement Glass jug Royal Doulton

SHOPPING FOR ONE

SHOPPING LIST

This is a list of the vegetables that are most useful in the single cook's kitchen. However, these will vary from person to person and week to week according to individual taste and availability of produce. A guide has been given as to how much of each vegetable you will require for one week's meals. This will vary, of course, depending on how you plan to use them and on personal taste.

☐ Iceberg/Butter lettuce – 1 lettuce. Hydroponic lettuces last longer as they are still growing when you buy them and will continue to grow if kept in a plastic food bag in the crisper section of the refrigerator. If hydroponic lettuces are not available, ordinary lettuce will last for 4-5 days if kept in an airtight container or sealed plastic food bag in the crisper section of the refrigerator. Try some of the other lettuce varieties, such as radicchio, cos and mignonette (lollo rosso), for added variety.

☐ Carrots – 3-4 medium carrots should be sufficient for 1 week. The best way to store carrots is to wrap them in absorbent kitchen paper and place in a plastic food bag in the crisper section of the refrigerator. Wrapped in this way they last for weeks. Carrots are used in salads, stir-fries, baked dishes and as an accompaniment.

☐ Tomatoes – Buy either 3-4 large tomatoes or a punnet of cherry tomatoes depending on how you plan to use them.
Ripe tomatoes will keep in the refrigerator for up to 1 week. Wrap cut tomatoes in plastic food wrap and store in the refrigerator.

☐ Cucumber – 1 small. Store in a plastic food bag in the crisper section of the refrigerator.

☐ Celery – ¹/₂ bunch. Store in a plastic food bag or wrap in plastic food wrap.

☐ Peppers – 1 green pepper and 1 red pepper. Store in the crisper section of the refrigerator. Wrap cut peppers in plastic food wrap. They are great in salads and stir-fries.

☐ Mushrooms – 100 g/3¹/₂ oz button, cup or flat mushrooms. Store in a cloth or brown paper bag in the refrigerator. If stored in plastic, mushrooms sweat and spoil quickly.

☐ Zucchini (courgettes) – 2-3 should be sufficient for one week. Store in a plastic food bag in the crisper section of the refrigerator. Zucchini (courgettes) are delicious raw in salads and in stir-fries, baked dishes, pasta sauces, soups or as an accompaniment.

☐ Onions – Choose a selection of white, brown and red onions. If stored in a cool, dark, dry place onions will keep for 1-2 months. Store cut onions, wrapped in plastic food wrap, in the refrigerator.

☐ Sprouts – 1 punnet or bag. There are a number of sprout varieties available, the most popular being alfalfa and bean sprouts. To save wastage, you might like to grow your own sprouts – seeds are available at health food stores. Keep sprouts in a plastic food bag or the container in which you purchased them.

☐ Snow peas (mangetout)/sugar snap peas/beans – 60-125 g/2-4 oz. Store in a well-ventilated plastic food bag in the crisper section of the refrigerator. Sealed bags cause these vegetables to sweat and spoil quickly.

☐ Spring onions – ¹/₂ bunch. Store unwashed, wrapped in

plastic food wrap or in a plastic food bag in the crisper section of the refrigerator. Spring onions are a good substitute for onions in dishes such as salads, stir-fries, baked dishes, sauces and soups.

☐ Potatoes – 3-4 average-sized potatoes or 8-10 baby potatoes. Store in a cool, dark, dry place with plenty of ventilation. Baby new potatoes are excellent for salads and as an accompaniment.

☐ Broccoli – 1 small head. Stored in a well-ventilated plastic food bag in the crisper section of the refrigerator, broccoli keeps for 4-5 days. The drier broccoli is, the longer it will keep.

☐ Pumpkin – 250 g/8 oz piece. Cut pumpkin, wrapped in plastic food wrap, will keep in the refrigerator for 4-5 days. Uncut pumpkins can be kept for up to 2 months. The storage life of pumpkin makes it a good standby ingredient for making such dishes as pumpkin soup.

☐ Cauliflower – 1 small head. Stored in a plastic food bag in the crisper section of the refrigerator, cauliflower will keep for 4-5 days.

☐ Leeks – 1 small. Leeks are a good alternative to onions or spring onions in your cooking. Store, wrapped in plastic food wrap or in a plastic food bag, in the crisper section of the refrigerator.

☐ Selection of fresh fruit such as apples (green and/or red), citrus fruits, stoned fruit, melons. Choose fruits that are in season, as not only do they taste the best but they are also the cheapest.

☐ Selection of herbs, such as parsley, basil, mint, coriander and dill. You might like to grow your own herbs to save having to buy more than you can use.

SHOPPING NOTES

The following hints will help you make the most of food shopping.

✎ If shopping for one is new to you, you may feel uncomfortable asking for one chop or one fillet of fish. Just remember that many butchers, greengrocers, fishmongers and delicatessens have customers asking for just enough for one or two.

✎ Ask your butcher and fishmonger to do the difficult and time-consuming jobs, such as boning and filleting.

✎ In the supermarket you will find many products that are made or packaged for one.

✎ Do not buy large quantities just because an item is on special. Remember that if you buy 2 kg/ 5 lb of minced meat and each serving is 125 g/4 oz, you have enough meat for sixteen meals!

✎ Fruit and vegetables in season are of the best quality and are the least expensive.

✎ Look for salad mixes in greengrocers and supermarkets. These are a mixture of lettuce leaves and you buy the quantity that you require. This gives you variety without having to buy a number of different lettuces, which may only be partially used.

✎ Buy eggs in packs of six.

✎ Buy wine for cooking in casks or flagons. It keeps well and is readily available to use in your cooking. Leftover bottled wine can be frozen in ice cube trays, then stored in sealed freezer bags. When 1 or 2 tablespoons of wine are required in cooking, just drop in one or two wine cubes.

✎ Before going shopping, plan menus so that you buy economically.

✎ Keep a variety of storecupboard ingredients on hand so that you can quickly and easily prepare a meal without having to go shopping.

MAKE A MEAL FROM A CAN

Canned salmon, tuna, beans or soup all make tasty bases for quick and easy meals. This selection of recipes demonstrates the versatility of a can.

SPEEDY SALMON LASAGNE

The tomato supreme used in this recipe consists of tomatoes, celery, peppers and various spices. If it is unavailable, you can use canned tomatoes instead.

Makes 1 serving
Oven temperature 180°C, 350°F, Gas 4

- ☐ 2 teaspoons vegetable oil
- ☐ 1 zucchini (courgette), sliced
- ☐ 4 instant lasagne sheets, cooked
- ☐ 100 g/3^1/$_2$ oz canned pink salmon, drained and flaked
- ☐ 310 g/10 oz canned tomato supreme mixed with ^{1}/$_2$ teaspoon dried mixed herbs
- ☐ ^{1}/$_2$ cup/60 g/2 oz grated tasty cheese (mature Cheddar)

1 Heat oil in a small nonstick frying pan and cook zucchini (courgette) over a medium-high heat for 3-4 minutes or until tender. Remove pan from heat and set aside.

2 Layer lasagne sheets, salmon, tomato supreme mixture, zucchini (courgette) and cheese into a greased, small ovenproof dish, finishing with a cheese layer.

3 Bake for 10-15 minutes or until cheese is melted and golden.

Serving suggestion: For a complete meal accompany with a crisp salad of lettuce, celery, red or green pepper and snow peas (mangetout).

Freeze it: This recipe makes a large serving. Leftover lasagne can be frozen in an airtight freezerproof container. Defrost in refrigerator overnight and reheat in the oven at 180°C/350°F/Gas 4 for 10 minutes or in microwave on HIGH (100%) for 2-3 minutes or until heated. You may wish to sprinkle the lasagne with a little extra grated tasty cheese (mature Cheddar) before reheating.

CHILLI BEANS

Makes 2 servings

- ☐ 2 teaspoons oil
- ☐ 1 small onion, finely chopped
- ☐ 1 cup/250 mL/8 fl oz canned tomato purée
- ☐ 1 cup/250 mL/8 fl oz chicken or vegetable stock
- ☐ 310 g/10 oz canned red kidney beans, rinsed and drained
- ☐ 1 tablespoon chilli sauce
- ☐ ^{1}/$_2$ teaspoon ground cumin

Heat oil in a nonstick frying pan and cook onion over a medium heat for 3-4 minutes or until soft. Stir in tomato purée, stock, beans, chilli sauce and cumin. Bring to simmering and simmer for 30 minutes or until mixture reduces and thickens.

Serving suggestions: These delicious beans can be served in many ways. You may like to try some of the following:

Place Chilli Beans on a bed of rice, top with grated cheese and serve with a salad.

Fill warm taco shells with Chilli Beans, shredded lettuce, chopped tomato and grated cheese.

Spoon Chilli Beans down the centre of a pitta bread, top with grated cheese, shredded lettuce, chopped tomatoes, cucumber and beetroot, and roll up.

Make nachos, place corn chips in an ovenproof dish, top with Chilli Beans and grated cheese. Heat in oven at 180°C/350°F/Gas 4 for 5-10 minutes or until heated and cheese melts. Serve with avocado slices or sour cream.

Use Chilli Beans as a filling for toasted sandwiches.

Freeze it: Leftover Chilli Beans can be frozen in an airtight freezerproof container or sealed freezer bag. Allow to defrost at room temperature for 2-3 hours and reheat in a saucepan over a medium heat. Or reheat, from frozen, in the microwave on HIGH (100%) for 3-4 minutes or until hot.

Square enamel plates Accoutrement

CHICKEN WITH MUSHROOMS

Makes 1 serving

- ☐ **2 teaspoons vegetable oil**
- ☐ **1 boneless chicken breast fillet, cut into small cubes**
- ☐ **6 button mushrooms, sliced**
- ☐ **2 tablespoons white wine**
- ☐ **¹/₂ cup/125 mL/4 fl oz canned cream of chicken soup**
- ☐ **¹/₄ cup/60 mL/2 fl oz milk**
- ☐ **2 teaspoons chopped fresh parsley**

1 Heat oil in a nonstick frying pan and cook chicken over a medium-high heat for 3-4 minutes or until just cooked.

2 Add mushrooms and cook for 2 minutes longer. Stir wine, soup and milk into chicken mixture, bring to the boil, then reduce heat and simmer for 5-8 minutes or until mixture reduces and thickens. Stir in parsley.

Serving suggestions: This quick chicken dish can be served in any of the following ways:

Spoon warm chicken mixture into a large vol-au-vent case and serve with a crisp green salad.

Spoon chicken mixture over hot fettuccine and toss. Serve with a salad of lettuce, tomatoes, red or green pepper and olives tossed in an Italian dressing.

Make a chicken and mushroom pie for a cold winter's night. Line an individual ovenproof dish with ready-rolled puff pastry, fill with cold chicken mixture and top with pastry. Brush top of pie with a little milk and bake at 200°C/400°F/Gas 6 for 15 minutes or until pastry is puffed and golden.

Chicken with Mushrooms is also a great filling for toasted sandwiches.

TASTY TUNA MACARONI

Makes 1 serving

- ☐ **75 g/2¹/₂ oz macaroni**
- ☐ **15 g/¹/₂ oz butter**
- ☐ **¹/₂ onion, chopped**
- ☐ **220 mL/7 fl oz canned tomato soup**
- ☐ **100 g/3¹/₂ oz canned tuna, drained and flaked**
- ☐ **¹/₄ cup/30 g/1 oz grated tasty cheese (mature Cheddar)**
- ☐ **freshly ground black pepper**

1 Cook macaroni in boiling water in a saucepan following packet directions. Drain, set aside and keep warm.

2 Melt butter in a small saucepan and cook onion over a medium heat for 3-4 minutes or until soft. Add tomato soup and cook for 1 minute longer. Stir in tuna and cook for 2-3 minutes longer or until heated. Mix in macaroni, tasty cheese (mature Cheddar) and season to taste with black pepper.

Serving suggestion: Sprinkle with Parmesan cheese and accompany with crusty bread.

Clockwise from left: Nachos made with Chilli Beans, Tasty Tuna Macaroni, Chicken with Mushrooms in Vol-au-Vent, Speedy Salmon Lasagne

MEALS WITHOUT MEAT

Many people now choose to eat one or two meals a week that do not contain meat. The recipes in this section fit the bill for those meatless days and are ideal for vegetarians.

Vegetable Patties with Avocado Sauce
(recipe page 26)

Plates Corso De Fiori Fork Bay Tree Marble Granite Art

Plate and bowl Corso De Fiori Cane table Home & Garden Glass Accoutrement Napkin Les Olivades

VEGETABLE PATTIES WITH AVOCADO SAUCE

*Served on rolls or pitta bread
with salad and hummus, these
patties are perfect for lunch.*

Makes 6 patties

- ☐ **315 g/10 oz canned butter beans, rinsed and drained**
- ☐ **1 small carrot, peeled and grated**
- ☐ **1¹/₂ cups/90 g/3 oz bread crumbs made from stale bread**
- ☐ **1 egg, lightly beaten**
- ☐ **2 tablespoons tomato sauce**
- ☐ **1 tablespoon snipped fresh chives**
- ☐ **freshly ground black pepper**
- ☐ **¹/₂ cup/60 g/2 oz dried bread crumbs**
- ☐ **1 tablespoon oil**

AVOCADO SAUCE
- ☐ **¹/₄ cup/60 g/2 oz sour cream**
- ☐ **¹/₄ avocado, peeled and mashed**
- ☐ **1 teaspoon lemon juice**
- ☐ **pinch chilli powder**

1   To make patties, place half the beans in a bowl and mash. Add remaining beans, carrot, bread crumbs made from stale bread, egg, tomato sauce and chives. Season to taste with black pepper and mix to combine. Shape bean mixture into six patties, using wet hands. Roll patties in dried bread crumbs to coat, place on a tray or plate lined with plastic food wrap, cover and refrigerate for 30 minutes.

2   Heat oil in a nonstick frying pan and cook patties for 4-5 minutes each side.

3   To make sauce, place sour cream, avocado, lemon juice and chilli powder in a small saucepan and heat until just warm. Serve sauce with patties.

Serving suggestion: Accompany with a mixed green salad and a wholemeal roll.

Freeze it: Leftover patties can be frozen between sheets of plastic food wrap in an airtight freezerproof container or sealed freezer bag. Defrost patties at room temperature for 1¹/₂-2 hours and serve cold, or reheat in a nonstick frying pan over a medium heat for 3-4 minutes, or in the oven at 180°C/350°F/ Gas 4 for 4-5 minutes or until heated. Or defrost and reheat in the microwave. Defrost 1 pattie on DEFROST (30%) for 3-4 minutes, then heat on HIGH (100%) for 1-2 minutes.

MARINATED TOFU SALAD

Makes 1 serving

- ☐ **2 tablespoons soy sauce**
- ☐ **1 teaspoon oil**
- ☐ **¹/₄ teaspoon finely chopped fresh ginger**
- ☐ **2 teaspoons lemon juice**
- ☐ **1 teaspoon dry white wine (optional)**
- ☐ **125 g/4 oz tofu, cut into cubes**
- ☐ **4 lettuce leaves**
- ☐ **1 small tomato, cut into wedges**
- ☐ **15 g/¹/₂ oz snow pea sprouts or watercress**
- ☐ **1 small carrot, sliced**
- ☐ **1 teaspoon sesame seeds, toasted**

1   Place soy sauce, oil, ginger, lemon juice and wine in a small bowl. Add tofu and toss to coat. Set aside to marinate for 10-15 minutes.

2   Place lettuce, tomato, snowpea sprouts or watercress and carrot in a bowl. Drain tofu and reserve liquid. Add tofu to salad, toss to combine and sprinkle with sesame seeds. Serve reserved liquid as a dressing.

Serving suggestion: Accompany with wholegrain or rye bread.

*Above: Marinated Tofu Salad
Right: Harvest Hotpot, Vegetable Soup*

26

HARVEST HOTPOT

Makes 2 servings

- ☐ ¼ cup/60 g/2 oz pearl barley, washed
- ☐ 2 cups/500 mL/16 fl oz vegetable stock
- ☐ 2 teaspoons oil
- ☐ 1 leek, finely sliced
- ☐ 1 zucchini (courgette), chopped
- ☐ ½ red pepper, cut into thin strips
- ☐ 1 stalk celery, chopped
- ☐ 2 tomatoes, peeled and chopped
- ☐ ¼ teaspoon dried mixed herbs
- ☐ 1 tablespoon tomato paste (purée)
- ☐ 125 g/4 oz canned corn kernels, drained
- ☐ freshly ground black pepper

1 Place barley and stock in a small saucepan, bring to the boil, then reduce heat and simmer for 30 minutes or until barley is soft.

2 Heat oil in a small frying pan and cook leek until soft. Add leek, zucchini (courgette), red pepper, celery, tomatoes, mixed herbs and tomato paste (purée) to barley mixture, then bring to simmering and simmer for 5-6 minutes or until vegetables are soft. Stir in corn kernels and season to taste with black pepper.

Serving suggestion: Serve with crusty bread.

Vegetable Soup: The remaining hotpot can be made into a tasty soup by adding ¾ cup/185 mL/6 fl oz canned tomato soup and reheating over a medium heat for 10 minutes or until hot.

Soup Terrine Accoutrement Casserole Dish Accoutrement

VEGETABLE PERFECTION

How long should you cook vegetables? Use this handy cooking chart as a guide to cooking times. When boiling vegetables you should bring the water to the boil before adding the vegetables.

TIPS FOR MICROWAVING VEGETABLES

✧ Always cover vegetables during cooking with microwave-safe plastic food wrap or lid.

✧ Vegetables can also be cooked in a plastic food bag. This saves on cleanup and your cooking vessel is always the right size. To cook in a bag, place prepared vegetables in bag, expel as much air as possible, twist bag loosely just above vegetables and place bag in microwave with end tucked under vegetables to secure. Cook for required time.

✧ Round, shallow dishes are the best containers to cook in. Vegetables cook more evenly in a round dish, and a shallow dish has less space above the food so less air. Air tends to toughen food during cooking in the microwave.

✧ Vegetables with the same cooking times can be cooked together in the same dish. Calculate the cooking time by weighing all the vegetables and use the cooking time chart as your guide.

✧ Vegetables with different cooking times can be cooked together by placing the longest cooking vegetables (such as potatoes, carrots and pumpkin) around the edge of a microwave-safe dish or plate. Then arrange the vegetables with the next longest cooking time (such as Brussels sprouts and sweet potato) inside the first circle. Finally place the vegetables with the shortest cooking time (such as broccoli and peas) in the centre of the dish. Add cooking times for each vegetable to give the total cooking time.

✧ Do not add salt to vegetables before cooking. Salt draws water out of food and so causes it to toughen during cooking.

✧ Pierce the surface of whole vegetables with skin left on, such as potatoes, before cooking.

✧ The water that clings to the vegetables after washing is usually sufficient for cooking the vegetables in the microwave. However, some vegetables, such as beans, need a little extra water to achieve best results. Adding water will increase the cooking time.

✧ Frozen vegetables can be cooked straight from the freezer in a dish or plastic food bag without added water. The ice that melts during cooking is all the moisture that is necessary.

✧ Stand vegetables for 2-3 minutes after cooking, to allow the heat to be evenly distributed and cooking to be completed.

COOK IT RIGHT

VEGETABLE	MICROWAVE	BOIL	STEAM
ASPARAGUS	5 stalks, 1-2 minutes (stand for 2 minutes before serving)	8-10 minutes	15 minutes
BEANS	60 g/2 oz with 2 teaspoons water, 2-3 minutes (stand 2-3 minutes before serving)	6-8 minutes	15 minutes
BROCCOLI (broken into florets)	60 g/2 oz, 1-2 minutes	5-8 minutes	10-15 minutes
BRUSSELS SPROUTS	75 g/2$\frac{1}{2}$ oz, 1-2 minutes	10-15 minutes	10 minutes
CABBAGE (shredded)	45 g/1$\frac{1}{2}$ oz, 45 seconds-1 minute	3-5 minutes	5-10 minutes
CARROTS (sliced)	60 g/2 oz, 3-4 minutes	12-15 minutes	20-25 minutes
CAULIFLOWER (broken into florets)	60 g/2 oz, 2-3 minutes	6-8 minutes	10-12 minutes
CORN (on the cob)	1 whole cob, 3-4 minutes	10-12 minutes	15 minutes
EGGPLANT (AUBERGINES)	60 g/2 oz, 2-4 minutes	Not suitable	Not generally used
PEAS	60 g/2 oz, 1-2 minutes	10-12 minutes	15 minutes
POTATOES (whole)	1 medium, 3 minutes	25-40 minutes	30-45 minutes
PUMPKIN (chopped)	60 g/2 oz, 3-4 minutes	20-30 minutes	35-45 minutes
SNOW PEAS (MANGETOUT)	60 g/2 oz, 30 seconds-1 minute	3 minutes	5 minutes
SPINACH (shredded)	4 leaves, 1-2 minutes	5 minutes	10 minutes
ZUCCHINI (COURGETTES)	60 g/2 oz, 1-2 minutes	5 minutes	5-10 minutes

MAKE A MEAL FROM AN EGG

Eggs are a natural fast food – in fact they take less time to cook than most prepared convenience foods – and are full of goodness and taste.

Egg in a Nest, Golden Flat Omelette, One-serve Quiches, Egg Roll

GOLDEN FLAT OMELETTE

Makes 1 serving

- [ ] 1 teaspoon polyunsaturated oil
- [ ] 2 spring onions, chopped
- [ ] 1 clove garlic, crushed
- [ ] 2 eggs
- [ ] 1 tablespoon water
- [ ] 30 g/1 oz ham, chopped
- [ ] 1/2 tomato, chopped
- [ ] 2 teaspoons chopped fresh coriander or parsley
- [ ] 1/4 cup/30 g/1 oz grated tasty cheese (mature Cheddar)
- [ ] freshly ground black pepper
- [ ] 15 g/1/2 oz butter

1   Heat oil in a small frying pan and cook spring onions and garlic over a medium heat for 3-4 minutes or until soft. Remove from heat.

2   Whisk eggs and water until well blended. Add spring onion mixture, ham, tomato, coriander or parsley and cheese, and mix well. Season to taste with black pepper.

3   Melt butter in a small frying pan, pour in egg mixture and cook over a medium heat, stirring, and lifting edges with a fork or spatula until mixture is almost firm on top. Cook for 30 seconds longer or until browned on the bottom. Place under a preheated medium grill and cook until top is firm and browned. Serve immediately.

Serving suggestion: Serve with a crisp green salad and a slice of toasted, white or wholemeal bread. Or you might like to serve a salad of tomatoes and basil.

EGG ROLL

Makes 1 roll
Oven temperature 180°C, 350°F, Gas 4

- [ ] 1 plain or wholemeal roll
- [ ] 2 teaspoons French mustard
- [ ] 1 teaspoon polyunsaturated oil
- [ ] 3 button mushrooms, sliced
- [ ] 1/4 small onion, chopped
- [ ] 15 g/1/2 oz ham, cut into strips
- [ ] freshly ground black pepper
- [ ] 1 egg
- [ ] 2 tablespoons grated tasty cheese (mature Cheddar)

1   Cut a slice from the top of roll, set aside and reserve. Scoop out the centre, leaving a thin shell; reserve crumbs for another use. Spread the inside of roll with mustard.

2   Heat oil in a nonstick frying pan and cook mushrooms and onion over a medium heat for 2-3 minutes or until onion softens. Add ham and cook for 2 minutes longer. Place mixture in cavity of roll and season to taste with black pepper.

3   Break egg into a small bowl and slide into roll. Sprinkle with cheese and replace top of roll. Place on a baking tray and cook for 25 minutes or until egg white is firm.

Spinach and Bacon Roll: Replace French mustard with tomato paste (purée), and mushrooms and onion with 1 chopped spinach leaf and season to taste with nutmeg. Prepare as in recipe.

Hot Salami Roll: Replace French mustard with tomato paste (purée), and mushrooms and ham with 30 g/1 oz hot salami. Prepare as in recipe. Sprinkle with cheese and 1 teaspoon toasted pine nuts before cooking.

Vase and glass Home & Garden *Blue and white plates and salt and pepper shakers* Accoutrement *Knife and square dish* The Bay Tree

ONE-SERVE QUICHES

Serve a quiche unaccompanied as a light meal, or with a crisp green salad for something more substantial. Delicious served hot, warm or cold.

Makes 6 quiches
Oven temperature 200°C, 400°F, Gas 6

- [ ] **315 g/10 oz prepared shortcrust pastry**

BACON FILLING
- [ ] **2 rashers bacon, chopped**
- [ ] **4 spring onions, finely chopped**
- [ ] **1 small red pepper, finely chopped**
- [ ] **1 clove garlic, crushed**
- [ ] **1 tablespoon snipped fresh chives**
- [ ] **freshly ground black pepper**
- [ ] **2 eggs**
- [ ] **³/₄ cup/185 mL/6 fl oz cream (double)**
- [ ] **¹/₄ cup/30 g/1 oz grated fresh Parmesan cheese**
- [ ] **¹/₂ cup/60 g/2 oz grated tasty cheese (mature Cheddar)**

1   Roll out pastry to 3 mm/¹/₈ in thickness and line six greased 10 cm/ 4 in individual flan tins. Line pastry with nonstick baking paper and weigh down with uncooked rice. Bake for 10 minutes, then remove rice and paper and bake for 10-15 minutes longer or until pastry is lightly browned. Set aside to cool.

2   To make filling, cook bacon, spring onions, red pepper and garlic in a nonstick frying pan over a medium heat for 3-4 minutes or until bacon is crisp. Remove from heat, stir in chives and season to taste with black pepper. Set aside to cool. Place eggs, cream and Parmesan cheese in a bowl and whisk to combine.

3   Divide red pepper mixture between pastry cases. Spoon egg mixture over, sprinkle with tasty cheese (mature Cheddar) and cook for 15-20 minutes or until firm.

Freeze it: Quiches are great freezer standbys. To freeze, layer cooked quiches between sheets of freezer wrap and place in an airtight freezerproof container or sealed freezer bag. Defrost quiches at room temperature for 30-60 minutes. Place quiches on a baking tray and reheat in oven at 180°C/350°F/Gas 4 for 5-8 minutes or until heated.

EGG IN A NEST

Makes 1 serving
Oven temperature 180°C, 350°F, Gas 4

- [ ] **1 rasher bacon, chopped**
- [ ] **¹/₂ small leek, sliced**
- [ ] **1 clove garlic, crushed**
- [ ] **¹/₂ small red pepper, cut into strips**
- [ ] **1 small zucchini (courgette), cut into strips**
- [ ] **2 teaspoons chopped fresh basil**
- [ ] **freshly ground black pepper**
- [ ] **1 egg**
- [ ] **¹/₄ cup/30 g/1 oz grated tasty cheese (mature Cheddar)**

1   Cook bacon, leek and garlic in a nonstick frying pan over a medium-high heat for 3-4 minutes or until bacon is crisp. Add red pepper and zucchini (courgette) and cook for 3-4 minutes longer. Stir in basil and season to taste with black pepper.

2   Spoon mixture into a small ovenproof dish and form a depression in the centre. Break egg into a small bowl and then slide into depression in vegetable mixture. Sprinkle with cheese and bake for 5-8 minutes or until the white is set.

Serving suggestion: Serve with crusty bread.

ADAPTING RECIPES

Most recipe books contain recipes for four, six or even eight servings, which can be frustrating for the single cook. However, with a few simple pointers – using the following recipes as a guide – you will find that it is easier than you thought to adapt a favourite recipe.

SALMON CROQUETTES FOR FOUR

- ☐ 3 large potatoes, cooked and mashed
- ☐ 1 onion, grated
- ☐ 440 g/14 oz canned pink salmon, drained and flaked
- ☐ 1 teaspoon Dijon-style mustard
- ☐ 2 tablespoons mayonnaise
- ☐ 1 egg, beaten
- ☐ freshly ground black pepper
- ☐ 200 g/6^1/2 oz cheese-flavoured biscuits, crushed
- ☐ polyunsaturated oil for cooking

1 Combine potato, onion, salmon, mustard, mayonnaise and egg, and season to taste with black pepper. Shape mixture into croquettes and roll in biscuit crumbs to coat.

2 Heat oil in a frying pan and cook croquettes over a medium heat until golden brown. Drain on absorbent kitchen paper.

SALMON CROQUETTES FOR ONE

- ☐ 1 medium potato, cooked and mashed
- ☐ ^{1}/4 small onion, grated
- ☐ 125 g/4 oz canned pink salmon, drained and flaked
- ☐ ^{1}/4 teaspoon Dijon-style mustard
- ☐ 2 tablespoons mayonnaise
- ☐ freshly ground black pepper
- ☐ 60 g/2 oz cheese-flavoured biscuits, crushed
- ☐ polyunsaturated oil for cooking

1 Combine potato, onion, salmon, mustard and mayonnaise, and season to taste with black pepper. Shape mixture into croquettes and roll in biscuit crumbs to coat.

2 Heat oil in a frying pan and cook croquettes over a medium heat until golden brown. Drain on absorbent kitchen paper.

Cook's tip: As it is difficult to use only part of an egg when reducing this recipe the egg was omitted and extra mayonnaise was used as a binding agent. Depending on the potatoes you use, you may find that the mixture is a little sticky. If this occurs, just add a little self-raising flour to the salmon to make it easier to handle.

LAMB CURRY FOR SIX

- ☐ 1 kg/2 lb cubed lamb
- ☐ seasoned flour
- ☐ 2 tablespoons vegetable oil
- ☐ 2 onions, chopped
- ☐ 1 clove garlic, crushed
- ☐ 1 teaspoon grated fresh ginger
- ☐ 1 tablespoon dry white wine
- ☐ 2 teaspoons soy sauce
- ☐ 1 teaspoon curry paste
- ☐ 2 teaspoons curry powder
- ☐ $^1/_2$ teaspoon ground turmeric
- ☐ $^1/_2$ teaspoon ground cumin
- ☐ 1 cup/250 mL/8 fl oz beef stock

1 Toss meat in flour to coat. Shake off excess flour. Heat half the oil in a large saucepan and cook meat in batches over a medium-high heat until browned on all sides. Remove meat from pan and drain on absorbent kitchen paper.

2 Heat remaining oil in saucepan and cook onions for 3-4 minutes or until soft. Add garlic, ginger, wine, soy sauce, curry paste, curry powder, turmeric and cumin and cook for 1 minute longer.

3 Return meat to pan, add stock, bring to the boil, then reduce heat and simmer, covered, for 1 hour or until meat is tender and mixture has thickened.

JUST-FOR-ONE LAMB CURRY

- ☐ 155 g/5 oz cubed lamb
- ☐ seasoned flour
- ☐ 3 teaspoons vegetable oil
- ☐ $^1/_2$ onion, chopped
- ☐ $^1/_2$ clove garlic, crushed
- ☐ $^1/_4$ teaspoon grated fresh ginger
- ☐ 2 teaspoons dry white wine
- ☐ $^1/_2$ teaspoon soy sauce
- ☐ $^1/_4$ teaspoon curry paste
- ☐ $^1/_2$ teaspoon curry powder
- ☐ pinch ground turmeric
- ☐ pinch ground cumin
- ☐ $^1/_3$ cup/90 mL/3 fl oz beef stock

1 Toss meat in flour to coat. Shake off excess flour. Heat half the oil in a small saucepan and cook meat over a medium-high heat until browned on all sides. Remove meat from pan and drain on absorbent kitchen paper.

2 Heat remaining oil in saucepan and cook onion for 3-4 minutes or until soft. Add garlic, ginger, wine, soy sauce, curry paste, curry powder, turmeric and cumin and cook for 1 minute longer.

3 Return meat to pan with stock, bring to the boil, then reduce heat and simmer, covered, for 1 hour or until meat is tender and mixture has thickened.

Serving suggestion: Serve with boiled or steamed white rice and vegetables of your choice.

Top left: Salmon Croquettes
Left: Lamb Curry

33

Chair Corso De Fiori Stained glass window Stained Glass Overlay Napkin and placemat Les Olivades Cutlery The Bay Tree

LIGHT MEALS

The recipes in this section are for those times when you feel like a very quick or light meal. Many can become a more substantial meal simply by adding a salad or vegetables, and bread or potatoes. Some of the recipes make more than one serving so that you can freeze the remainder.

Tortellini with Creamy Tomato Sauce (recipe page 36)

TORTELLINI WITH CREAMY TOMATO SAUCE

Makes 1 serving

- ☐ **155 g/5 oz tortellini**
- ☐ **1 tablespoon grated fresh Parmesan cheese**
- ☐ **basil leaves**

CREAMY TOMATO SAUCE
- ☐ **2 teaspoons oil**
- ☐ **1 small onion, finely chopped**
- ☐ **1 clove garlic, crushed**
- ☐ **$^3/_4$ cup/185 mL/6 fl oz canned tomato soup**
- ☐ **1 tablespoon red wine**
- ☐ **2 teaspoons finely chopped fresh basil**
- ☐ **$^1/_4$ cup/60 mL/2 fl oz cream (double)**
- ☐ **freshly ground black pepper**

1 Cook tortellini in boiling water in a saucepan following packet directions. Drain, set aside and keep warm.

2 To make sauce, heat oil in a small saucepan and cook onion over a medium heat for 3-4 minutes or until soft. Add garlic, soup, wine and basil, bring to simmering and simmer for 5 minutes. Remove pan from heat, stir in cream and season to taste with black pepper. Spoon sauce over tortellini, top with Parmesan cheese and basil leaves.

Serving suggestion: Accompany with crusty Italian bread.

Leftovers tip: Any leftover sauce can be made into a tasty soup. Place remaining sauce, $^1/_2$ cup/125 mL/4 fl oz milk and $^1/_4$ cup/60 mL/2 fl oz of water in a saucepan or microwave-safe jug and heat over a medium heat until hot, or cook in microwave on HIGH (100%) for 2-3 minutes.

Glass plates Villeroy & Boch Stained glass Stained Glass Overlay

Fast Fried Rice, Fruity Rice Salad

FAST FRIED RICE

Makes 1 serving

- ☐ 2 teaspoons oil
- ☐ 2 spring onions, finely chopped
- ☐ 1 stalk celery, finely chopped
- ☐ 1 egg, lightly beaten
- ☐ 2 slices ham, finely chopped
- ☐ 125 g/4 oz canned corn kernels, drained
- ☐ $1/3$ cup/75 g/$2^1/2$ oz rice, cooked
- ☐ 2 teaspoons soy sauce

1 Heat oil in a nonstick frying pan and cook spring onions and celery over a medium heat for 3-4 minutes or until onion softens. Remove onion mixture from pan and set aside. Pour egg into pan and cook for 2 minutes or until set. Leaving omelette in pan and using an egg slice, chop omelette into small pieces.

2 Add onion mixture, ham, corn, rice and soy sauce to pan and stir to combine. Cook for 1 minute longer or until heated.

FRUITY RICE SALAD

This is a great recipe for using leftovers.

Makes 1 serving

- ☐ $1/3$ cup/75 g/$2^1/2$ oz rice, cooked
- ☐ 1 small apple, cored and chopped
- ☐ 2 tablespoons sultanas
- ☐ $1/4$ green pepper, chopped
- ☐ 2 tablespoons sunflower seeds
- ☐ 2 teaspoons finely chopped fresh coriander or parsley

ORANGE DRESSING
- ☐ $1/4$ cup/60 mL/2 fl oz freshly squeezed orange juice
- ☐ 1 teaspoon finely grated orange rind
- ☐ $1/2$ teaspoon finely chopped fresh ginger
- ☐ 1 teaspoon honey, warmed

1 Place rice, apple, sultanas, green pepper, sunflower seeds and coriander or parsley in a bowl and toss to combine.

2 To make dressing, place orange juice, orange rind, ginger and honey in a screwtop jar and shake to combine. Pour dressing over rice salad. Serve immediately.

BASICALLY BREAD

Wholemeal, white or rye bread, whatever the type, is a nutritious and satisfying food that can be enjoyed by everyone. Use these easy ideas to make wonderful bread snacks, or simply make a sandwich using your favourite bread and filling.

SALMON TOASTIES

This easy snack uses store-cupboard ingredients and is just as delicious made with canned tuna.

Makes 2 toasties
Oven temperature 200°C, 400°F, Gas 6

- ☐ **155 g/5 oz canned pink salmon, drained**
- ☐ **¹/₄ cup/60 g/2 oz sour cream**
- ☐ **2 teaspoons lemon juice**
- ☐ **2 teaspoons chopped fresh dill or parsley**
- ☐ **freshly ground black pepper**
- ☐ **15 g/¹/₂ oz butter**
- ☐ **4 slices bread, crusts removed**

1   Place salmon, sour cream, lemon juice, dill or parsley and black pepper to taste in a small bowl and mix to combine. Lightly butter bread on one side.

2   Spread half of the salmon mixture over unbuttered side of 2 slices of bread. Cover with remaining bread slices, buttered side up. Secure sides with wooden cocktail sticks or toothpicks.

3   Place on a greased baking tray and bake for 10 minutes or until bread is crisp and golden.

Cook's tip: If you do not have any sour cream, mayonnaise or natural yogurt can be used instead.

HAM AND CORN TRIANGLES

Makes 4 triangles
Oven temperature 180°C, 350°F, Gas 4

- ☐ **2 slices bread**
- ☐ **15 g/¹/₂ oz butter, melted**

CORN TOPPING
- ☐ **60 g/2 oz canned creamed corn**
- ☐ **1 spring onion, finely chopped**
- ☐ **1 slice canned pineapple, chopped**
- ☐ **1 slice ham, finely chopped**
- ☐ **¹/₂ cup/60 g/2 oz grated tasty cheese (mature Cheddar)**

1   Cut each slice of bread in half diagonally and brush both sides with butter. Place bread triangles on a baking tray and bake for 5 minutes or until crisp.

2   Top toasted triangles with corn, spring onion, pineapple, ham and cheese. Bake for 5 minutes or until cheese is melted and golden.

From left: Open Focaccia Sandwich, Ham and Corn Triangles, Salmon Toasties

OPEN FOCACCIA SANDWICH

For something different use any of your favourite breads, spreads, meats and vegetables to make this sandwich.

Makes 1 serving

- ☐ **1 piece focaccia bread, halved and buttered**
- ☐ **4 slices roast beef or lamb**
- ☐ **¼ avocado, peeled and sliced**
- ☐ **4 cherry tomatoes, sliced**
- ☐ **1 teaspoon finely chopped fresh rosemary (optional)**
- ☐ **4 slices Swiss cheese**
- ☐ **freshly ground black pepper**

To assemble sandwiches, top focaccia with beef or lamb, avocado and tomatoes then sprinkle with rosemary and top with Swiss cheese. Season to taste with black pepper.

Toasted Focaccia Sandwich: Toasted, this sandwich is a wonderful light evening meal. Toast focaccia slices under a preheated grill on both sides before buttering. Prepare as in recipe then place under a preheated medium grill and cook for 3-4 minutes or until heated and cheese is melted.

Cook's tip: Why not use a bread that you have not tried before to make this sandwich. There are many breads available from bread shops, supermarkets and delicatessens. You might try using white bread, wholemeal bread, wholegrain bread, rye bread, sandwich rolls, baguettes/ French rolls, pitta bread, crispbread or bagels. Remember that bread freezes well so you can buy a whole loaf and any leftover can be frozen to use at a later date.

MAKING THE MOST OF BREAD

Bread is not fattening – it is low in fat and sugar and contains significant amounts of protein, minerals, complex carbohydrates (starch), vitamins (especially thiamin) and dietary fibre. Stored at room temperature bread will stay fresh for 3-4 days. It is best to keep it in a well-ventilated bread box or bin, and in hot, humid weather keep your bread in the refrigerator.

For the single person, the freezer is the ideal place to keep bread. It is easy to remove one or two slices as you require them. When separated, slices will defrost in 5-10 minutes at room temperature. If you wish to toast the bread, you can place it, frozen, into the toaster. Freezing will not affect the nutritional value of bread.

Basket Home & Garden Tray and plates Accoutrement Coaster, placemat and napkin, jug and glass Waterford Wedgwood

TUNA CANNELLONI

Makes 1 serving
Oven temperature 180°C, 350°F, Gas 4

- ☐ **1 packet white sauce mix**
- ☐ **185 g/6 oz canned tuna, drained**
- ☐ **2 teaspoons snipped fresh chives**
- ☐ **1 tablespoon mayonnaise**
- ☐ **4 cooked cannelloni tubes**
- ☐ **¹/₄ cup 30 g/1 oz grated tasty cheese (mature Cheddar)**

1 Make up white sauce according to packet directions. Place tuna, chives, mayonnaise and 2 tablespoons of white sauce in a bowl and mix to combine.

2 Fill cannelloni tubes with tuna mixture, and place tubes in a small greased ovenproof dish. Pour remaining white sauce over cannelloni and sprinkle with cheese. Bake for 10 minutes or until heated and cheese is melted.

Serving suggestion: Accompany with a salad of lettuce, tomatoes, spring onions and black olives tossed with a vinaigrette dressing.

Microwave it: This dish can also be cooked in the microwave. Prepare as in the recipe but instead of baking in the oven cook in the microwave on HIGH (100%) for 3-4 minutes or until heated.

Tuna Cannelloni

40

TURKEY TRIANGLES

Makes 4 triangles
Oven temperature 220°C, 425°F, Gas 7

- [ ] **155 g/5 oz prepared puff pastry**

TURKEY FILLING
- [ ] **4 slices smoked turkey, chopped**
- [ ] **2 tablespoons sour cream**
- [ ] **1 tablespoon cranberry sauce**
- [ ] **2 teaspoons snipped fresh chives**
- [ ] **freshly ground black pepper**

1 Roll out pastry to 3 mm/^{1}/$_8$ in thickness and cut into four 12.5 cm/5 in squares.

2 To make filling, place turkey, sour cream, cranberry sauce and chives in a small bowl and mix to combine. Place a spoonful of filling in the centre of each pastry square. Fold opposite pastry corners together to form a triangle. Brush edges with a little water and press together, using a fork to seal and make a decorative edge. Place on a greased baking tray and bake for 15 minutes or until pastry is puffed and golden.

Bacon and Swiss Triangles: Chop 2 rashers bacon and cook in a frying pan until crisp. Remove from pan and drain on absorbent kitchen paper. Mix bacon with ^{1}/$_2$ cup/60 g/2 oz grated Swiss cheese. Make triangles as in recipe.

Freeze it: It is worth making double the quantity of this recipe so that you can freeze the triangles to have on hand for snacks and light meals. Freeze triangles in an airtight freezerproof container or sealed freezer bag. Reheat in oven at 180°C/350°F/Gas 4 for 10-15 minutes or until heated.

Turkey Triangles

Fabric and napkin Les Olivades Sauce dish Accoutrement

Plate Home & Garden Table Corso De Fiori

CHEESY CHICKEN PASTIES

Keep a store of these delicious pasties in your freezer – you will always have a tasty light meal to hand.

Makes 10 pasties
Oven temperature 200°C, 400°F, Gas 6

- ☐ **375 g/12 oz prepared shortcrust pastry**
- ☐ **2 tablespoons milk**

CHICKEN FILLING
- ☐ **30 g/1 oz butter**
- ☐ **1 clove garlic, crushed**
- ☐ **2 boneless chicken breast fillets, chopped**
- ☐ **8 small button mushrooms, sliced**
- ☐ **6 stalks asparagus, chopped**
- ☐ **2 tablespoons sour cream**
- ☐ **$^1/_2$ cup/60 g/2 oz grated tasty cheese (mature Cheddar)**
- ☐ **2 tablespoons grated fresh Parmesan cheese**
- ☐ **1 tablespoon chopped fresh parsley**
- ☐ **freshly ground black pepper**

1   Roll out pastry to 3 mm/$^1/_8$ in thickness and, using an upturned saucer as a guide, cut out ten 13 cm/5$^1/_4$ in circles. Set aside.

2   To make filling, melt 15 g/$^1/_2$ oz butter in a frying pan and cook garlic and chicken over a medium-high heat for 3-4 minutes or until chicken is cooked. Remove chicken mixture from pan and set aside to cool. Melt remaining butter in pan and cook mushrooms and asparagus over a high heat for 3-4 minutes or until asparagus is tender crisp. Remove mushroom mixture from pan and set aside to cool.

3   Place chicken mixture, mushroom mixture, sour cream, tasty cheese (mature Cheddar), Parmesan cheese, parsley and black pepper to taste in a bowl and mix to combine. Place a spoonful of mixture in the centre of each pastry round and brush edge of pastry with a little water. Draw edges together over top of filling, press to seal and crimp edges with fingertips to form a fluted pattern.

4   Brush pastry parcels with a little milk, place on a greased baking tray and bake for 20-25 minutes or until golden brown.

Serving suggestion: Serve unaccompanied for a snack, or with a salad for a light meal.

SATAY STIR-FRY

Prepared satay sauce is available from supermarkets and specialty food shops.

Makes 1 serving

- ☐ **2 teaspoons oil**
- ☐ **1 small onion, cut into eighths**
- ☐ **1 small carrot, cut into thin strips**
- ☐ **60 g/2 oz snow peas (mangetout), trimmed and sliced diagonally into 5 cm/2 in lengths**
- ☐ **$^1/_4$ red pepper, cut into thin strips**
- ☐ **2 spinach leaves, finely shredded**
- ☐ **2 tablespoons satay sauce**

Chair, plate and bowl Corso De Fiori

- [ ] **1 tablespoon chopped roasted unsalted peanuts**

1 Heat oil in a nonstick frying pan and cook onion over a medium heat for 3-4 minutes or until soft.

2 Add carrot, snow peas (mangetout), red pepper and spinach to pan and stir-fry for 3-4 minutes or until vegetables are just tender. Stir in satay sauce and peanuts.

Serving suggestion: Serve with rice or vermicelli noodles.

Left: Pasta Salad
Below: Satay Stir-fry

Plate, salt and pepper holder and small bowl Corso De Fiori

PASTA SALAD

The dressing for this salad is also delicious tossed through a green lettuce salad.

Makes 1 serving

- [ ] **60 g/2 oz pasta spirals, cooked**
- [ ] **60g/2oz snow peas (mangetout), trimmed and blanched**
- [ ] **$^1/_4$ red pepper, cut into thin strips**
- [ ] **6 cherry tomatoes, halved**
- [ ] **4 slices salami, cut into strips**

MUSTARD DRESSING
- [ ] **2 tablespoons mayonnaise**
- [ ] **1 tablespoon French dressing**
- [ ] **$^1/_2$ teaspoon wholegrain mustard**

1 To make dressing, place mayonnaise, French dressing and mustard in a bowl, and whisk to combine.

2 Place pasta, snow peas (mangetout), red pepper, cherry tomatoes and salami in a serving bowl, spoon dressing over.

Serving suggestion: Serve with a crusty bread roll.

Above: Cheesy Chicken Pasties

SOUPS

Served with crusty bread, a bagel or a sesame seed roll and followed by fruit and cheese or a crisp green salad, soups make a quick, satisfying meal.

CHILLED TOMATO SOUP

A delightfully refreshing, low-calorie soup, perfect for a summer lunch. Serve with Tomato Minted Ice Cubes if desired.

Makes 2 servings

- ☐ **2 teaspoons olive oil**
- ☐ **1 small onion, chopped**
- ☐ **1 clove garlic, crushed**
- ☐ **2 cups/500 mL/16 fl oz vegetable stock**
- ☐ **2 tablespoons finely chopped fresh mint**
- ☐ **220 g/7 oz canned peeled tomatoes, drained**
- ☐ **1 zucchini (courgette), grated**
- ☐ **freshly ground black pepper**

1   Heat oil in a saucepan and cook onion and garlic over a medium heat for 3-4 minutes or until onion is soft. Add stock and mint, bring to the boil, then reduce heat and simmer for 5 minutes.

2   Place tomatoes and stock mixture in a food processor or blender and process until smooth. Stir in zucchini (courgette) and season to taste with black pepper. Chill well before serving.

Serving suggestion: Place three Tomato Minted Ice Cubes (see recipe) in a serving bowl and pour chilled soup over.

Freeze it: Half the soup can be frozen in an airtight freezerproof container. Defrost at room temperature for 2-3 hours and then rechill or defrost in the refrigerator overnight.

TOMATO MINTED ICE CUBES

- ☐ **fresh mint leaves**
- ☐ **³/₄ cup/185 mL/6 fl oz tomato juice**
- ☐ **³/₄ cup/185 mL/6 fl oz water**

Place a mint leaf in each space of an ice cube tray. Mix together tomato juice and water and pour into ice cube tray. Freeze.

Cook's tip: This quantity of ice cubes will be enough for 4 servings. Remove ice cubes from tray and store in a sealed freezer bag.

SPICY PUMPKIN SOUP

A less spicy soup can be made by omitting the coriander, cumin and chilli powder. Instead, stir in 2 teaspoons chopped fresh parsley with the cream.

Makes 2 servings

- ☐ **2 teaspoons vegetable oil**
- ☐ **1 small onion, chopped**
- ☐ **1 clove garlic, crushed**
- ☐ **¹/₄ teaspoon ground coriander**
- ☐ **¹/₄ teaspoon ground cumin**
- ☐ **pinch chilli powder**
- ☐ **500 g/1 lb pumpkin, peeled, seeded and chopped**
- ☐ **1¹/₂ cups/375 mL/12 fl oz chicken stock**
- ☐ **2 tablespoons cream (double)**
- ☐ **freshly ground black pepper**

1   Heat oil in a saucepan and cook onion over a medium heat for 3-4 minutes or until soft. Add garlic, coriander, cumin and chilli powder and cook for 1 minute longer.

2   Add pumpkin and stock to pan, bring to the boil, then reduce heat and simmer for

Creamy Broccoli Soup, Spicy Pumpkin Soup

15-20 minutes or until pumpkin is tender. Remove pan from heat and set aside to cool slightly. Place pumpkin and cooking liquid in batches in a food processor or blender and process until smooth.

3   Return soup to a clean saucepan, stir in cream, season to taste with black pepper and cook over a medium heat, without boiling, until heated.

Serving suggestion: Accompany soup with crusty bread and follow with a crisp garden salad.

Freeze it: Half the soup can be frozen in an airtight freezerproof container, omitting cream. Defrost soup at room temperature for 2-3 hours or until liquid. Add cream and reheat in a saucepan over a medium heat for 4-5 minutes or until heated. Or place frozen soup in a microwave-safe jug and cook on HIGH (100%) for 4-5 minutes or until liquid, stir in cream and cook on HIGH (100%) for 1-2 minutes longer.

Cook's tip: Instead of using a food processor to purée the soup, you can remove the cooked pumpkin from the stock and mash it, using a potato masher or fork, then mix in cooking liquid and complete as in recipe.

CREAMY BROCCOLI SOUP

Makes 2 servings

- [ ] **2 teaspoons vegetable oil**
- [ ] **1 small onion, chopped**
- [ ] **2 cups/500 mL/16 fl oz chicken stock**
- [ ] **1 small potato, peeled and chopped**
- [ ] **185 g/6 oz broccoli florets**
- [ ] **1 tablespoon chopped fresh parsley**
- [ ] **freshly ground black pepper**

1   Heat oil in a saucepan and cook onion over a medium heat for 3-4 minutes or until soft. Add stock, potato and broccoli, bring to the boil, then reduce heat and simmer for 10-15 minutes or until potato is tender.

2   Transfer mixture to a food processor or blender and process until smooth.

3   Return soup to a clean saucepan, stir in parsley and season to taste with black pepper. Cook over a medium heat until heated.

Serving suggestion: Serve with a swirl of cream and accompany with a grilled cheese-topped bagel.

Freeze it: Half the soup can be frozen in an airtight freezerproof container. Defrost soup at room temperature for 2-3 hours or overnight in the refrigerator. Reheat in a saucepan over a medium heat, or place frozen soup in a microwave-safe jug and cook on HIGH (100%) for 6-7 minutes or until hot. Stir once during cooking.

CHICKEN AND CORN SOUP

Makes 2 servings

- [ ] **2 teaspoons vegetable oil**
- [ ] **1 small onion, sliced**
- [ ] **1 small potato, diced**
- [ ] **2 cups/500 mL/16 fl oz chicken stock**
- [ ] **pinch ground cumin**
- [ ] **90 g/3 oz cooked chicken, chopped**
- [ ] **125 g/4 oz canned corn kernels**
- [ ] **freshly ground black pepper**
- [ ] **2 teaspoons finely chopped fresh parsley**

1   Heat oil in a saucepan and cook onion over a medium heat for 3-4 minutes or until soft. Add potato and stock, bring to the boil, then reduce heat and simmer for 10-15 minutes or until potato is tender.

2   Remove onion and potato, using a slotted spoon, and place in a food processor or blender and process until smooth. Return potato purée to stock mixture and whisk to combine. Stir in chicken and corn and cook over a low heat until heated. Season to taste with black pepper.

Serving suggestion: Sprinkle with parsley and serve with a slice of crusty bread.

Freeze it: Half the soup can be frozen in an airtight freezerproof container. Defrost in the refrigerator overnight. Reheat in a saucepan over a medium heat until hot, or place frozen soup in a microwave-safe jug and cook on HIGH (100%) for 6-7 minutes or until hot. Stir once during cooking.

Cook's tip: This soup is best eaten within 4 weeks of freezing. After this time the potato can cause the soup to become watery.

Chilled Tomato Soup, Chicken and Corn Soup

MICROWAVE IT

Fish, chicken, vegetables and sauces are all quick and easy to cook in the microwave, and even more so when you are cooking just for one.

CREAMY MACARONI CHEESE

Macaroni cheese just for one? The microwave makes this quick and easy – and, you use only one dish.

Makes 1 serving
Microwave power setting HIGH (100%)

- ☐ **60 g/2 oz macaroni**
- ☐ **¹/₂ cup/125 mL/4 fl oz water**
- ☐ **30 g/1 oz butter**
- ☐ **3 teaspoons flour**
- ☐ **¹/₂ teaspoon dry mustard powder**
- ☐ **¹/₂ cup/125 mL/4 fl oz milk**
- ☐ **¹/₄ cup/30 g/1 oz grated tasty cheese (mature Cheddar)**
- ☐ **2 spring onions, finely chopped**
- ☐ **1 slice ham, chopped**
- ☐ **1 tablespoon finely chopped parsley**

1   Place macaroni, water and butter in casserole dish and cook, uncovered, fc 6-7 minutes or until macaroni is tender.

2   Stir in flour, mustard and milk and coo for 1-2 minutes or until thickened. Stir i cheese, spring onions, ham and parsle and cook for 1 minute longer.

QUICKEST EVER BAKED POTATO

When cooked in a conventional oven a baked potato takes 45-60 minutes, but in the microwave the same potato takes 3-5 minutes to cook and is just as delicious.

Makes 1 serving
Microwave power setting HIGH (100%)

- ☐ **1 large potato, scrubbed**
- ☐ **2 tablespoons natural yogurt**
- ☐ **1 teaspoon finely chopped parsley**
- ☐ **1 teaspoon finely snipped chives**
- ☐ **freshly ground black pepper**

1   Pierce skin of potato several times with a skewer or fork. Cook potato for 4-5 minutes or until tender.

2   Cut top from potato and, using a teaspoon, scoop out flesh leaving a 1 cm/³/₄ in shell. Place potato flesh, yogurt, parsley, chives and black pepper to taste in a small bowl. Mash, then spoon back into potato shell. Cook for 30-45 seconds.

Sauce boat and plate The Bay Tree

CHICKEN BAKE

Makes 1 serving
Microwave power setting HIGH (100%)

- [ ] **1 boneless chicken breast fillet, chopped**
- [ ] **1 small potato, sliced**
- [ ] **30 g/1 oz butter**
- [ ] **1 spring onion, chopped**
- [ ] **1 clove garlic, crushed**
- [ ] **2 teaspoons flour**
- [ ] **¼ cup/60 mL/2 fl oz chicken stock**
- [ ] **2 teaspoons chopped fresh parsley**
- [ ] **2 teaspoons snipped fresh chives**
- [ ] **1½ tablespoons sour cream**
- [ ] **freshly ground black pepper**
- [ ] **15 g/½ oz grated tasty cheese (mature Cheddar)**
- [ ] **pinch cayenne pepper**

1 Place chicken in a microwave-safe dish, cover with microwave-safe plastic food wrap and cook for 1-2 minutes or until just cooked.

2 Place potato in a microwave-safe shallow dish. Dot with 15 g/½ oz butter, cover with microwave-safe plastic food wrap and cook for 3-4 minutes or until tender. Place remaining butter, spring onion and garlic in a microwave-safe jug and cook for 20-30 seconds or until butter melts. Stir in flour, then stock, parsley and chives. Cook for 1 minute, stirring every 20 seconds, or until sauce thickens. Stir in sour cream and season to taste with black pepper.

3 Layer potato, chicken and sauce in an individual microwave-safe dish. Sprinkle with cheese and cayenne pepper and cook for 2-3 minutes or until heated through.

Serving suggestion: Accompany with a crisp salad and a slice of crusty bread.

Left: Fish Fillet with Hollandaise Sauce, Creamy Macaroni Cheese
Above: Quickest Ever Baked Potato, Chicken Bake

Fork The Design Store Salad bowl, round dish and plate The Bay Tree Table Oz Design

FISH FILLET WITH HOLLANDAISE SAUCE

Hollandaise Sauce is also wonderful spooned over boiled, steamed or microwaved vegetables.

Makes 1 serving
Microwave power setting HIGH (100%)

- [ ] **15 g/½ oz butter**
- [ ] **4 teaspoons lemon juice**
- [ ] **4 teaspoons dry white wine**
- [ ] **1 x 125-155 g/4-5 oz white fish fillet, such as perch, whiting or ling**

HOLLANDAISE SAUCE
- [ ] **45 g/1½ oz butter**
- [ ] **1 egg yolk**
- [ ] **1 teaspoon lemon juice**
- [ ] **freshly ground black pepper**

1 Place butter in a small microwave-safe dish and cook for 15 seconds or until melted. Combine butter, lemon juice and wine. Place fish in a shallow microwave-safe dish and pour butter mixture over. Cover dish loosely with microwave-safe plastic food wrap and cook for 2-3 minutes or until fish flakes when tested with a fork. Set aside and keep warm.

2 To make sauce, place butter in a microwave-safe dish and cook for 15 seconds or until melted. Place egg yolk and lemon juice in a microwave-safe jug and whisk to combine. Gradually whisk in butter. Cook sauce on MEDIUM (50%) for 40 seconds, whisking every 15 seconds, or until sauce thickens. Season to taste with black pepper. Spoon sauce over fish and serve immediately.

Serving suggestion: Delicious with baby new potatoes, green beans and carrots.

MAKE A MEAL FROM A POTATO

Don't just think of a potato as an accompaniment to a meal. These delicious recipes show you how a potato can be a meal in itself.

POTATO PANCAKE

Makes 1 serving

- ☐ 1 large potato, peeled and grated
- ☐ 2 tablespoons flour
- ☐ 1 egg, lightly beaten
- ☐ 1 tablespoon grated fresh Parmesan cheese
- ☐ 1 tablespoon finely snipped fresh chives
- ☐ freshly ground black pepper
- ☐ 2 teaspoons vegetable oil

Squeeze as much moisture as possible from potato. Place potato, flour, egg, Parmesan cheese and chives in a bowl and mix to combine. Season to taste with black pepper. Heat oil in a small nonstick frying pan. Place mixture into pan and spread to cover base. Cook pancake for 4-5 minutes each side or until golden.

Serving suggestions: Serve pancake topped with: sour cream, tasty cheese (mature Cheddar) and freshly ground black pepper; chopped chicken and avocado; or pan-cooked onion, tomato, mushrooms and chopped fresh parsley or chives.

SPICY POTATO PIZZA

Makes 1 serving

- ☐ 1 large potato, cooked and mashed
- ☐ 15 g/¹/₂ oz butter
- ☐ 1 tablespoon grated tasty cheese (mature Cheddar)
- ☐ 1 small tomato, sliced
- ☐ 3 slices hot salami
- ☐ 4 button mushrooms, sliced
- ☐ ¹/₄ green pepper, chopped
- ☐ ¹/₂ cup/60 g/2 oz grated mozzarella cheese

1 Place potato, butter and tasty cheese (mature Cheddar) in a small bowl and mix to combine. Place potato mixture into a greased nonstick frying pan and spread to cover base.

2 Arrange tomato, salami, mushrooms and green pepper over potato. Sprinkle with mozzarella cheese and cook over a medium heat until potato is crisp and golden. Place under a preheated low grill and cook for 8-10 minutes or until cheese is melted and golden.

Cook's tip: Instant potato makes a quick and easy substitute.

POTATO AND CHICKEN CURRY

Makes 1 serving

- ☐ 2 teaspoons vegetable oil
- ☐ 1 small onion, chopped
- ☐ 1 boneless chicken breast fillet, cut into strips
- ☐ 1 large potato, peeled and cubed
- ☐ 1¹/₂ cups/375 mL/12 fl oz chicken stock
- ☐ 1-2 teaspoons curry paste
- ☐ 90 g/3 oz broccoli florets
- ☐ 90 g/3 oz cauliflower florets
- ☐ 1 teaspoon cornflour blended with 2 teaspoons water
- ☐ 3-4 teaspoons natural yogurt or sour cream

1 Heat oil in a small saucepan and cook onion for 2-3 minutes or until soft. Add chicken and cook for 4-5 minutes or until chicken is browned. Add potato, stock and curry paste, bring to simmering and simmer for 7-8 minutes.

2 Add broccoli and cauliflower and simmer for 4-5 minutes longer or until vegetables are tender. Stir in cornflour mixture and cook until sauce is slightly thickened. Just prior to serving, stir in yogurt or sour cream.

Serving suggestion: Serve curry with rice and poppadums. Poppadums can be cooked in the microwave. Place poppadums on absorbent kitchen paper and cook on HIGH (100%) for 1-2 minutes or until puffed.

POTATO TORTILLA

In Spain a tortilla is a flat omelette. In Mexico, thin pancakes made of corn meal are also called tortillas.

Makes 1 serving

- ☐ 1 potato, peeled and sliced
- ☐ 15 g/1¹/₂ oz butter
- ☐ ¹/₂ small red onion, finely sliced
- ☐ 1 rasher bacon, chopped
- ☐ ¹/₄ red pepper, cut into thin strips
- ☐ 1 clove garlic, crushed
- ☐ 2 eggs, lightly beaten
- ☐ 2 teaspoons chopped fresh parsley
- ☐ freshly ground black pepper
- ☐ ¹/₄ cup/30 g/1 oz grated tasty cheese (mature Cheddar)

1 Bring a small saucepan of water to the boil, add potato slices and cook for 5-6 minutes or until just tender. Drain well.

2 Melt half the butter in a small frying pan and cook onion, bacon, red pepper and garlic over a medium heat for 3-4 minutes or until onion softens. Remove from pan and set aside.

3 Place eggs, parsley and black pepper to taste in a bowl and whisk to combine. Melt remaining butter in pan and layer potato slices and onion mixture into pan. Pour egg mixture over and cook over a medium heat for 5-8 minutes or until egg mixture is just set. Sprinkle with cheese and cook under a preheated high grill for 2-3 minutes or until cheese melts.

Potato Pancake, Spicy Potato Pizza, Potato and Chicken Curry, Potato Tortilla

HEALTHY LIFESTYLE

A balanced diet and exercise are the keys to a healthy lifestyle. Use these hints and tips to maintain or establish a good diet and an exercise program.

MAKE THE MOST OF MEALS

One of the best things about being a single cook is that you are the only one you have to please.

• If you want to buy food on a day-to-day basis you can eat what you feel like on that day.

• Experiment with new recipes and enjoy flavours that you have not experienced before.

• When planning a meal, keep in mind your lifestyle, age and the amount of physical activity you do.

CONVENIENCE FOODS

Convenience foods appear to be an attractive alternative to a home-cooked meal for those short of time or who do not enjoy cooking. However, the wrong choice of takeaway or convenience foods can lead to an unbalanced diet.

• Fast foods such as oriental vegetable stir-fries, lean hamburgers with salad, barbecued chicken without skin, pasta in noncream sauces, and freshly squeezed juices are good choices. Hot chips, deep-fried chicken and seafood, spring rolls, thick shakes and soft drinks are best avoided.

• Canned and frozen foods often contain high levels of salt and sugar, however with a little planning and the addition of fresh fruit and vegetables at the meal these foods can be included in your diet. Many manufacturers are now producing salt-free, reduced-salt, low-salt and reduced-fat products, so look out for these when buying canned and frozen foods.

• The recipes in this book are quick to prepare and nutritious. Ten minutes cooking in the kitchen instead of 5 minutes waiting in the takeaway shop will benefit your tastebuds, your nutritional needs and your pocket.

DON'T SKIP MEALS

Skipping meals leads to:
• snacking on junk food because you are hungry. Most junk food is high in kilojoules (calories) and fat;
• missing valuable nutrients required daily; and
• a slowing of your metabolism, which makes it harder to burn body fat.

6 TIPS FOR HEALTHY EATING

The following tips will help you plan a balanced diet:
• Use herbs and spices to give flavour and to help cut down on salt.
• Keep a good balance between food consumption and daily exercise.
• Wherever possible use polyunsaturated margarines and oils to help keep cholesterol at a moderate level. Fatty foods such as potato crisps and chips, bacon, mayonnaise, fried and pastry-based takeaway foods, toasted muesli, chocolate and peanut butter, should only be eaten occasionally.
• A small amount of sugar does no harm. However, cutting sugar out of tea and coffee and leaving it off your breakfast cereal will help cut your daily kilojoule (calorie) intake.
• Eating more fruit, vegetables, breads and cereals, fibre and complex carbohydrates helps digestion and provides the body with a preferred energy source.
• Trim all visible fat from meat before cooking and remove skin from chicken before eating.

EXERCISE

Regular exercise is an important part of a healthy lifestyle. It not only contributes to weight loss but also:
• relieves tension
• alleviates mild depression
• helps joint flexibility
• helps to improve muscle strength
• increases the rate of your body metabolism
• helps lower blood cholesterol levels
• helps improve sleeping patterns
• helps prevent osteoporosis
• helps prevent bone fractures

Exercising should be enjoyable, so choose a sport that you like, is convenient, fits in with your lifestyle and that you can do for at least 30 minutes three times a week.
You may like to incorporate your exercise into your daily routine:
• Walk part of the way to work instead of catching the bus.
• Walk up the stairs instead of taking the lift.
• Walk to the shops instead of driving.
• Take the dog for a walk regularly.
• Undertake the housework with vigour and energy.

DESSERTS

For those times when you feel you deserve a treat, here is a selection of dessert recipes. Many make more than one serving so that you can freeze the remaining portions to have on hand when time is short.

Mini Berry Cakes
(recipe page 54)

DOUBLE CHOCOLATE SOUFFLE

Makes 1 soufflé
Oven temperature 190°C, 375°F, Gas 5

- ☐ 2 tablespoons cream (double)
- ☐ 60 g/2 oz dark chocolate, chopped
- ☐ 1 egg, separated
- ☐ 1 tablespoon caster sugar
- ☐ 30 g/1 oz white chocolate, finely chopped

1   Place cream and dark chocolate in a heatproof bowl and stir over simmering water until chocolate melts and mixture is smooth. Whisk in egg yolk and set aside to cool.

2   Beat egg white until soft peaks form. Gradually add sugar, beating well after each addition until sugar has dissolved and mixture is thick and glossy. Mix white chocolate into chocolate mixture and then fold into egg white mixture. Spoon into a greased 1¹/₂ cup/375 mL/12 fl oz capacity soufflé dish and cook for 25-30 minutes or until well puffed. Serve immediately.

MINI BERRY CAKES

Makes 3
Oven temperature 180°C, 350°F, Gas 4

- ☐ 60 g/2 oz butter, softened
- ☐ ¹/₂ teaspoon vanilla essence
- ☐ ¹/₃ cup/75 g/2¹/₂ oz caster sugar
- ☐ 1 egg, separated
- ☐ ³/₄ cup/90 g/3 oz self-raising flour, sifted
- ☐ ¹/₄ cup/60 mL/2 fl oz milk
- ☐ 3 tablespoons drained canned blueberries

1   Place butter and vanilla essence in a mixing bowl and beat until light and fluffy. Add sugar a little at a time, beating well after each addition until mixture is creamy.

2   Add egg yolk and beat well. Fold flour and milk, alternately, into egg yolk mixture. Beat egg white until soft peaks form and fold into batter. Spoon half the batter into three greased large muffin tins or ³/₄ cup/ 185 mL/6 fl oz capacity ramekins, top with berries and spoon over remaining batter. Bake for 20-25 minutes or until cakes are cooked when tested with a skewer.

Serving suggestion: These cakes are wonderful served straight from their ramekins or turned out and served with whipped cream, ice cream or warm custard.

Freeze it: Freeze cakes individually in airtight freezerproof containers or sealed freezer bags. Defrost at room temperature for 1-1¹/₂ hours to serve as a morning or afternoon tea treat. To serve hot, remove cakes from freezer, wrap in absorbent kitchen paper and reheat in the microwave on HIGH (100%) for 1¹/₂ minutes.

Double Chocolate Soufflé, Brownie Torte

Soufflé dish Accoutrement Plate, cup and saucer Royal Doulton

RUM AND RAISIN
FRENCH TOAST

Makes 4 triangles

- ☐ **1 egg**
- ☐ **2 teaspoons dark rum**
- ☐ **1 tablespoon caster sugar**
- ☐ **2 thick slices raisin loaf, halved diagonally**
- ☐ **30 g/1 oz butter**

1   Whisk egg, rum and sugar together and pour into a shallow dish. Place bread into egg mixture and allow to soak, turning, for 1-2 minutes, or until bread has absorbed all of the egg.

2   Melt butter in a nonstick frying pan and cook bread over a medium-high heat for 2 minutes each side or until crisp and golden brown.

Serving suggestion: Serve with a sprinkling of brown sugar and scoops of vanilla ice cream.

Leftovers tip: The remaining raisin bread can be stored in the freezer until required and is delicious toasted for breakfast. Why not try Raisin French Toast for breakfast? Use the above recipe, but omit the rum and serve with maple syrup, golden syrup or honey.

BROWNIE TORTE

Makes a 20 cm/8 in round torte
Oven temperature 180°C, 350°F, Gas 4

- ☐ **125 g/4 oz dark chocolate, roughly chopped**
- ☐ **45 g/1¹/₂ oz butter, chopped**
- ☐ **1 egg**
- ☐ **¹/₄ cup/60 g/2 oz caster sugar**
- ☐ **¹/₂ teaspoon vanilla essence**
- ☐ **2 tablespoons flour, sifted**
- ☐ **60 g/2 oz slivered almonds**
- ☐ **60 g/2 oz milk chocolate, roughly chopped**

1   Place dark chocolate and butter in a heatproof bowl over a saucepan of simmering water and heat, stirring, for 5 minutes or until chocolate melts and mixture is smooth. Set aside to cool.

2   Place egg, sugar and vanilla essence in a bowl and beat until mixture is thick and creamy. Beat in chocolate mixture, then fold in flour, almonds and milk chocolate. Spoon mixture into a lightly greased and lined 20 cm/8 in sandwich tin and bake for 15-20 minutes or until cooked when tested with a skewer.

Serving suggestion: Serve with vanilla ice cream as a dessert or cut into thin wedges and serve as a special treat with coffee.

Freeze it: Cut torte into serving portions and freeze in airtight freezerproof containers or sealed freezer bags. Defrost at room temperature for 30-60 minutes. If cutting from frozen, slice torte with a knife dipped in hot water. The torte will defrost more quickly.

Cook's tip: Freezing nuts prevents them from going rancid. So if you only use small quantities of nuts, occasionally, this is a good way to keep them. Nuts – shelled, whole or chopped – can be frozen, in airtight freezerproof containers or sealed freezer bags. Be sure to expel all excess air before sealing. They will last up to six months in the freezer, however if salted and spiced their freezer life will be only about three months. They can be used straight from the freezer; there is no need to defrost first.

Rum and Raisin French Toast

BLACKBERRY AND APPLE CRUMBLE

Makes 2 serves
Oven temperature 180°C, 350°F, Gas 4

- [ ] **2 tablespoons rolled oats**
- [ ] **1 tablespoon soft brown sugar**
- [ ] **1 tablespoon flour**
- [ ] **$1/4$ teaspoon ground mixed spice**
- [ ] **15 g/$1/2$ oz butter**
- [ ] **185 g/6 oz drained canned blackberries**
- [ ] **250 g/8 oz drained canned apple slices**
- [ ] **$1^1/2$ tablespoons sugar**
- [ ] **$1/2$ teaspoon ground cinnamon**

1   Combine oats, brown sugar, flour and mixed spice in a bowl. Rub in butter, using fingertips, until mixture resembles coarse bread crumbs.

2   Combine blackberries, apple, sugar and cinnamon and spoon into two $3/4$ cup/185 mL/6 fl oz capacity ramekins or soufflé dishes. Sprinkle with oat mixture and cook for 10-15 minutes or until topping is golden and fruit heated.

Serving suggestion: Accompany with natural yogurt or whipped cream.

Leftovers tip: The second serving of this dessert is delicious cold for breakfast, or reheat it and eat as a snack or dessert. Reheat in a preheated oven at 180°C/350°F/Gas 4 for 8-10 minutes.

EASY PEAR STRUDEL

Makes 1 serving
Oven temperature 200°C, 400°F, Gas 6

- [ ] **1 tablespoon finely chopped dried apricots, soaked in 2 teaspoons brandy**
- [ ] **125 g/4 oz canned pears, drained**
- [ ] **1 tablespoon sugar**
- [ ] **$1/4$ teaspoon ground cinnamon**
- [ ] **$1/4$ teaspoon ground cloves**
- [ ] **2 sheets filo pastry**
- [ ] **15 g/$1/2$ oz butter, melted**
- [ ] **2 teaspoons soft brown sugar**

1   Drain any liquid from apricots. Place apricots, pears, sugar, cinnamon and cloves in a bowl and toss to combine. Set aside.

2   Brush one sheet of pastry with butter, sprinkle with a little brown sugar and top with second pastry sheet. Brush pastry with butter, sprinkle with remaining brown sugar and fold in half to form a rectangle. Spoon fruit mixture down centre of pastry. Fold in short ends and roll up. Place strudel on a greased baking tray, brush with remaining butter and bake for 10-15 minutes or until golden brown.

Serving suggestion: Serve with a scoop of vanilla or butterscotch ice cream or a dollop of natural yogurt. Delicious hot or cold.

Cook's tip: Any drained canned fruit can be used to make this dessert. Why not try apple, blackberries, strawberries, apricots or cherries – for these variations the dried apricots can be omitted.

GOLDEN BANANAS

Try this recipe using peeled, sliced apple instead of the banana. Apple will take 5-8 minutes to cook.

Makes 1 serving

- [ ] **15 g/$1/2$ oz butter**
- [ ] **3 teaspoons soft brown sugar**
- [ ] **1 tablespoon orange juice**
- [ ] **2 teaspoons dark rum**
- [ ] **1 banana, thickly sliced**

Melt butter in a small nonstick frying pan. Add sugar, orange juice and rum and stir over a medium heat until sugar dissolves. Add banana and cook for 3-4 minutes longer or until heated and banana is tender.

Serving suggestion: Delicious with whipped cream or vanilla ice cream.

Microwave it: To cook this recipe in the microwave, place all the ingredients in a microwave-safe dish, cover and cook on HIGH (100%) for 1-2 minutes or until heated and banana is tender.

Berry and Apple Crumble, Golden Bananas, Easy Pear Strudel, Berry Waffles

BERRY WAFFLES

If you do not have a waffle maker you can still enjoy waffles. Simply buy frozen waffles, toast them, make the sauce and serve as suggested in this recipe.

Makes 5 waffles

- ☐ $1/2$ cup/60 g/2 oz flour
- ☐ $1/2$ cup/60 g/2 oz self-raising flour
- ☐ 1 tablespoon icing sugar
- ☐ $1/2$ teaspoon ground cinnamon
- ☐ $1/2$ cup/125 mL/4 fl oz milk
- ☐ $1/2$ cup/125 mL/4 fl oz buttermilk or milk
- ☐ 90 g/3 oz butter, melted
- ☐ 1 egg, separated
- ☐ 200 g/6$1/2$ oz canned strawberries, drained and puréed

1 Sift together flour, self-raising flour, icing sugar and cinnamon into a mixing bowl.

2 Place milk, buttermilk or milk, butter and egg yolk in a bowl and whisk to combine. Make a well in the centre of flour mixture and mix in milk mixture until just combined. Beat egg white until soft peaks form, then fold into batter.

3 Cook batter in a preheated, greased waffle iron following manufacturer's instructions. Serve waffles with strawberry purée, vanilla ice cream and fresh strawberries if desired.

Freeze it: Freeze any remaining waffles between sheets of freezer wrap in an airtight freezerproof container or sealed freezer bag. Reheat straight from the freezer in the toaster, or in the oven at 180°C/350°F/Gas 4 for 5-8 minutes or until heated.

Buttermilk: Buttermilk is a low-fat milk, with a slightly acidic flavour. It has a thick consistency and smooth texture. Originally the soured liquid leftover from the butter-making process, buttermilk is now made from skim milk with the addition of special cultures to thicken it. Buttermilk is a good low-fat substitute for full-cream milk. It can be used in fruit drinks, soups, cakes, biscuits and breads. Milk can be used in place of buttermilk if you wish.

Plates and bowl Accoutrement

57

FREEZE IT

Freezing requires a little thought and planning, but with a bit of know-how, you can make the freezer your best friend.

FREEZING TIPS

• Freezer wrappings and containers should be nonporous so that flavours and moisture cannot escape from or enter the food.
• Remove as much air as possible from freezer bag or container before sealing.
• Before freezing, always label packages and containers with date and contents.
• Trim meat of excess fat. Lean meat has a longer freezer life than fatty meat.
• Freeze ingredients in serving sizes for one. This will avoid defrosting excess quantities. If you have company, another serving can easily be defrosted.
• Onion- and garlic-flavoured dishes may have to be seasoned again when reheating, as they lose their flavour after 3 months of freezing.

FOODS BEST NOT TO FREEZE

Eggs: Eggs in their shell or hard-boiled eggs do not freeze successfully; the shell can explode and the white toughens and becomes rubbery. Cooked dishes containing eggs, such as custards, may turn grainy when defrosted. Egg whites removed from their shell can be frozen for up to 3 months in a small freezerproof container. Thaw at room temperature before using.

Sauces: Emulsified sauces or sauces containing large quantities of cream, milk or eggs do not freeze well as they separate on defrosting. However, sauces such as tomato sauce will freeze well.

Salad vegetables: Because of their high water content most salad vegetables are not suitable for freezing. They lose their shape, wilt and go mushy on defrosting.

Dairy products, such as yogurt, sour cream, buttermilk and cottage cheese: The texture of these products changes on freezing and they cannot be restored to their original state when defrosted.

Jelly: Breaks down, and loses its shape and glossy appearance.

BEEF

Remove from original packaging and place in airtight freezerproof containers or sealed freezer bags in serving sizes. To defrost, leave in packaging and place in refrigerator overnight.

Freezer life:

Steak	6-8 months
Minced beef	1 month (seasoned)
	2 months (unseasoned)

LAMB AND VEAL

Remove from original packaging and place in airtight freezerproof containers or sealed freezer bags in serving sizes. Defrost in refrigerator in packaging overnight.

Freezer life:

Boneless	6-8 months
Chops	4-6 months
Cutlets	4-6 months

POULTRY

Remove from original packaging and place in airtight freezerproof containers or sealed freezer bags in serving sizes. To defrost, leave in

packaging and place in refrigerator overnight.

Freezer life:

Whole or pieces	4-6 months

PORK

Remove from original packaging and place in airtight freezerproof containers or sealed freezer bags in serving sizes. To defrost, leave in packaging and place in refrigerator overnight.

Freezer life:

Roasts	4-6 months
Chops/steaks	4-6 months

FRESH PASTA

Place in an airtight freezerproof container or sealed freezer bag. No need to defrost, just cook straight from the freezer.

Freezer life:

	1-2 months

STOCK

Cool completely, skim off fat, and place stock in an airtight freezerproof container or sealed freezer bag, or pour into ice block trays, freeze, then transfer to sealed freezer bags to store. Do not leave in trays as cubes will evaporate. Defrost in a saucepan over a low heat or in the microwave. When only a small quantity of stock is required, simply drop one or two frozen stock cubes into sauces,

casseroles, stews and soups.

Freezer life:

Vegetable and fish stocks	2 months
Beef and chicken stocks	6 months

SOUPS

Freeze soups before adding eggs or cream. Place soup in an airtight freezerproof container. Soups to be served hot: Defrost overnight in refrigerator, or at room temperature for 3-4 hours, and then reheat over a medium-low heat. Check seasonings before serving as freezing can alter flavour. Soups to be served cold: Defrost in refrigerator overnight and whisk to break up any remaining ice crystals.

Freezer life:	4 months

SAUCES

Place in an airtight freezerproof container. Defrost over a very low heat or in a bowl over a saucepan of simmering water, whisking constantly for a smooth texture. Or defrost in refrigerator overnight.

Freezer life:	4 months

BREAD/BUNS/ROLLS

Wrap in aluminium foil and package in sealed freezer bags. Defrost in wrapping at room

temperature for 1-2 hours or in the refrigerator overnight. Or heat from frozen in aluminium foil in oven at 180°C/350°F/Gas 4 for 10-15 minutes.

Freezer life:

Rolls/Buns	2 months
Loaves	4 months

PASTRY

Wrap tightly in plastic food wrap and then in aluminium foil or place in a sealed freezer bag. For un-cooked pastry cases, remove from tin after initial freezing, stack between sheets of freezer wrap and place in an airtight freezerproof container or sealed freezer bag. Allow block pastry to thaw completely at room temperature – this will take 2-3 hours – before rolling out. If you are not going to use the pastry immediately, thaw in packaging in the refrigerator overnight.

Freezer life:

Block	4 months
Pre-made cases	6 months

QUICHES

Open-freeze before wrapping in plastic food wrap or aluminium foil and place in an airtight freezerproof container or sealed freezer bag.
Thaw in wrapping in refrigerator overnight, or at room temperature for 2-4 hours.

Freezer life:	6-8 weeks

COOK AHEAD MEALS

One of the simplest ways to provide quick meals is to cook ahead and freeze. The following recipes have been specially chosen, as they freeze well.

Cheese and Salami Pizza
(recipe page 62)

Plate The Design Shop *Knife and fork* The Bay Tree *Tablecloth* Home & Garden

CHEESE AND SALAMI PIZZA

A great no-fuss snack or light meal.

Makes 2-3 servings
Oven temperature 190°C, 375°F, Gas 5

- [ ] $1^{1}/_{2}$ cups/185 g/6 oz flour
- [ ] $^{1}/_{2}$ cup/60 g/2 oz rye flour
- [ ] 1 teaspoon baking powder
- [ ] 1 teaspoon bicarbonate of soda
- [ ] 90 g/3 oz butter, melted
- [ ] $^{3}/_{4}$-1 cup/185-250 mL/6-8 fl oz buttermilk or milk
- [ ] 3 tablespoons tomato paste (purée)
- [ ] 2 tablespoons chopped fresh oregano or 2 teaspoons dried oregano
- [ ] freshly ground black pepper
- [ ] 125 g/4 oz thinly sliced salami
- [ ] 1 onion, thinly sliced
- [ ] 1 tomato, thinly sliced
- [ ] 45 g/$1^{1}/_{2}$ oz grated fresh Parmesan cheese
- [ ] 30 g/1 oz pine nuts
- [ ] 220 g/7 oz mozzarella cheese, grated

1   Sift together flour, rye flour, baking powder and bicarbonate of soda into a mixing bowl. Add butter and buttermilk or milk, and mix to form a soft dough.

2   Turn onto a floured surface and knead lightly until smooth. Press into a greased 22 x 30 cm/$8^{3}/_{4}$ x 12 in Swiss roll tin.

3   Spread dough with tomato paste (purée), sprinkle with oregano and black pepper to taste. Top with salami, onion, tomato, Parmesan cheese, pine nuts and mozzarella cheese. Bake for 15-20 minutes or until topping is golden and base is cooked.

Freeze it: Freeze in serving portions in airtight freezerproof containers or sealed freezer bags. Place frozen pizza on a baking tray and reheat in oven at 180°C/ 350°F/Gas 4 for 10-15 minutes or until hot. You may wish to add extra grated mozzarella cheese to the top of the pizza before reheating.

Crispy-based Pizza: Use a pitta bread for the base to make an extra-quick, crispy-based pizza.

CRUNCHY-TOPPED MOUSSAKA

Makes 4 servings
Oven temperature 180°C, 350°F, Gas 4

- ☐ 1 tablespoon olive oil
- ☐ 1 onion, chopped
- ☐ 2 cloves garlic, crushed
- ☐ 500 g/1 lb minced beef
- ☐ 1 teaspoon chopped fresh rosemary or $^1/_4$ teaspoon dried rosemary
- ☐ 440 g/14 oz canned peeled tomatoes, undrained and mashed
- ☐ 2 tablespoons tomato paste (purée)
- ☐ 2 teaspoons soy sauce
- ☐ $^1/_2$ cup/125 mL/4 fl oz red wine
- ☐ 1 teaspoon sugar
- ☐ $^1/_2$ teaspoon ground nutmeg
- ☐ 1 eggplant (aubergine), thinly sliced
- ☐ 6 slices bread, crusts removed
- ☐ 30 g/1 oz butter
- ☐ 2 tablespoons chopped fresh basil
- ☐ 2 tablespoons grated fresh Parmesan cheese

1 Heat oil in a nonstick frying pan and cook onion, garlic, beef and rosemary over a medium-high heat, stirring constantly, for 4-5 minutes or until beef is browned.

2 Stir in tomatoes, tomato paste (purée), soy sauce, wine, sugar and nutmeg. Cook, uncovered, over a medium heat for 20-25 minutes or until mixture thickens slightly.

3 Steam or microwave eggplant (aubergine) until just tender. Arrange layers of eggplant (aubergine) and mince mixture in four greased individual oven-to-freezer dishes, finishing with a layer of mince.

4 Spread bread with butter, cut into cubes and place on top of moussaka. Sprinkle with basil and Parmesan cheese and bake for 20-25 minutes or until heated through and golden brown.

Serving suggestion: Accompany with a crisp green salad.

Freeze it: Freeze in individual dishes in airtight freezerproof containers or sealed freezer bags. Defrost in refrigerator overnight. Reheat in oven at 180°C/350°F/ Gas 4 for 10-15 minutes or until hot. To reheat in the microwave, cook on MEDIUM (50%) for 4-5 minutes or until heated.

Cook's tip: You may find it more convenient to keep purchased, bottled, minced (ground) garlic, ginger and chilli in your refrigerator to have on hand whenever you require it for a recipe.

Glass and salad bowl/ The Design Shop Oval dish and napkins Accoutrement

Crunchy-topped Moussaka

VEAL GOULASH

Makes 4 servings

- ☐ 4 x 125 g/4 oz lean veal steaks, cut 1 cm/¹/₂ in thick
- ☐ 1¹/₂ tablespoons paprika
- ☐ 2 tablespoons flour
- ☐ freshly ground black pepper
- ☐ 1 tablespoon vegetable oil
- ☐ 2 onions, chopped
- ☐ 1 clove garlic, crushed
- ☐ 1 tablespoon tomato paste (purée)
- ☐ 3 tablespoons red wine
- ☐ ¹/₂ cup/125 mL/4 fl oz beef stock
- ☐ ¹/₄ cup/60 g/2 oz sour cream or natural yogurt

1   Trim meat of all visible fat and cut into 2 cm/³/₄ in cubes. Place paprika, flour and black pepper to taste in a plastic food bag, add meat and shake to coat meat evenly. Shake off excess flour.

2   Heat oil in a large saucepan and cook onion and garlic over a medium heat for 3-4 minutes or until onion softens. Combine tomato paste (purée), wine and stock. Stir stock mixture and meat into onion mixture. Bring to the boil, then reduce heat and simmer, covered, for 25-30 minutes or until meat is tender.

3   Remove from heat and stir one-third of the sour cream or yogurt into one serving of goulash. Serve immediately.

Serving suggestion: Serve with fettuccine and boiled, steamed or microwaved vegetables of your choice.

Freeze it: Omitting sour cream or yogurt, freeze remaining goulash in serving portions in airtight freezerproof containers or sealed freezer bags. Defrost, covered, in the refrigerator overnight. Reheat in a saucepan over a medium heat, stirring, until hot. To reheat in microwave, place in a microwave-safe dish and cook on HIGH (100%), stirring occasionally, for 2-3 minutes or until sauce boils. Add sour cream or yogurt just prior to serving.

Veal Goulash

Plate, bowl and small dish Corso De Fiori

DRY BEEF CURRY

Makes 2 servings

- ☐ **75 g/2¹/2 oz butter**
- ☐ **250 g/8 oz chuck steak, cubed**
- ☐ **1 small onion, cut into eighths**
- ☐ **1 red chilli, seeded and finely chopped**
- ☐ **1 clove garlic, crushed**
- ☐ **¹/2 teaspoon ground coriander**
- ☐ **¹/2 teaspoon ground turmeric**
- ☐ **¹/2 teaspoon ground cumin**
- ☐ **2 teaspoons ground garam masala**
- ☐ **¹/4 cup/60 mL/2 fl oz water**
- ☐ **1 large tomato, peeled and chopped**
- ☐ **¹/2 small cinnamon stick**
- ☐ **2 tablespoons natural yogurt**

1   Melt 60 g/2 oz butter in a large saucepan and cook steak in batches over a medium-high heat until browned on all sides. Remove from pan and set aside.

2   Melt remaining butter in pan and cook onion and chilli over a medium heat for 3-4 minutes or until soft. Stir in garlic, coriander, turmeric, cumin, and 1 teaspoon garam masala and cook for 1 minute longer.

3   Add water, tomato and cinnamon stick to pan. Return meat to pan. Bring to the boil, then reduce heat and simmer for 1¹/2 hours or until meat is tender.

4   Remove pan from heat. Divide into two portions and stir ¹/2 teaspoon garam masala and 1 tablespoon yogurt into one portion. Serve immediately.

Serving suggestion: Serve with extra yogurt and boiled or steamed white rice.

Freeze it: Freeze remaining serving of curry in an airtight freezerproof container or sealed freezer bag. Defrost in the refrigerator overnight. Reheat in a saucepan over a medium heat for 5-8 minutes or until hot. To reheat in the microwave, place in a microwave-safe dish, cover, and cook on HIGH (100%), stirring occasionally, for 3-4 minutes or until hot. Stir in ¹/2 teaspoon garam masala and 1 tablespoon yogurt just prior to serving.

Cook's tip: Individual dishes that can be used in the oven, microwave and freezer are invaluable in the single-cook's kitchen. A recipe that can be frozen and reheated in the one dish saves on time and washing up.

Dry Beef Curry

SECOND TIME AROUND

There are some dishes that do not easily convert to one serving. However, the clever use of leftovers will allow you to enjoy meals such as a roast chicken dinner while giving you an equally delicious, but completely different, meal the next day.

Pork Fillet with Chunky Apple, Pork Pie (recipes page 68)

Fabric Inmaterial Salt and pepper shakers Villeroy & Boch Knife and fork The Design Store Glass Home & Garden

Plate, canister, cup and saucer Corso De Fiori

PORK FILLET WITH CHUNKY APPLE SAUCE

Oven temperature 180°C, 350°F, Gas 4

- [ ] **15 g/^{1}/$_2$ oz butter**
- [ ] **1 tablespoon vegetable oil**
- [ ] **250 g/8 oz pork fillet**
- [ ] **1 tablespoon honey, warmed**
- [ ] **1 tablespoon white wine**
- [ ] **^{1}/$_2$ teaspoon ground allspice**

APPLE SAUCE
- [ ] **1 cooking apple, cored, peeled and roughly chopped**
- [ ] **2 tablespoons apple juice**
- [ ] **^{1}/$_2$ teaspoon grated orange rind**

1   Heat butter and 2 teaspoons oil in a nonstick frying pan and cook pork over a medium-high heat for 4-5 minutes or until browned on all sides. Combine honey, wine and allspice.

2   Heat remaining oil in a baking dish, add pork, pour honey mixture over and bake for 20 minutes or until cooked.

3   To make sauce, place apple, apple juice and orange rind in a small saucepan, bring to the boil, cover and simmer for 5 minutes or until apple is tender. Serve apple sauce with sliced pork.

Serving suggestion: Accompany with baby potatoes and steamed or microwaved cabbage tossed with a little butter and ^{1}/$_4$ teaspoon caraway seeds.

PORK PIE: Chop 1 rasher bacon and ^{1}/$_2$ small leek. Heat 2 teaspoons oil in a nonstick frying pan and cook bacon and leek over a medium heat for 2-3 minutes or until leek softens. Stir in 2 teaspoons flour and cook for 1 minute longer. Gradually mix in ^{1}/$_3$ cup/90 mL/3 fl oz beef stock and remaining apple sauce and cook, stirring constantly, until sauce boils and thickens. Cube remaining pork and stir into sauce with 2 teaspoons chopped fresh parsley and freshly ground black pepper to taste. Set aside to cool. Line a greased individual pie tin with prepared puff pastry, spoon cooled filling into pastry case and top with a pastry lid, pressing pastry edges together to seal. Brush with a little milk and cook in oven at 200°C/400°F/Gas 6 for 20 minutes or until pastry is puffed and golden.

BOWS WITH RICH TOMATO BASIL SAUCE

- [ ] **75 g/2^1/$_2$ oz bow pasta**

TOMATO BASIL SAUCE
- [ ] **2 teaspoons olive oil**
- [ ] **1 onion, sliced**
- [ ] **1 clove garlic, crushed**
- [ ] **3 tomatoes, peeled, seeded and chopped**
- [ ] **^{1}/$_2$ cup/125 mL/4 fl oz chicken stock**
- [ ] **1 tablespoon tomato paste (purée)**
- [ ] **1 tablespoon chopped fresh basil**
- [ ] **2 teaspoons chopped fresh parsley**
- [ ] **^{1}/$_2$ teaspoon sugar**
- [ ] **freshly ground black pepper**

1   Cook pasta in boiling water in a saucepan following packet directions. Drain, set aside and keep warm.

2   To make sauce, heat oil in a saucepan and cook onion and garlic over a medium heat for 3-4 minutes or until onion softens. Add tomatoes, stock, tomato paste (purée), basil, parsley and sugar and simmer for 10-15 minutes or until reduced and thickened. Season to taste with black pepper. Spoon sauce over pasta.

Serving suggestion: Sprinkle with a little grated fresh Parmesan cheese and extra chopped fresh basil. Accompany with a crusty baguette.

FRESH TOMATO SOUP: Chop 1 small carrot and 1 stalk celery. Place leftover sauce, 1 cup/250 mL/8 fl oz chicken stock, carrot and celery in a saucepan. Bring to simmering and simmer for 10-15 minutes or until carrot is tender. Season to taste with black pepper.

Serving suggestion: Serve with a buttered grilled bagel or pitta bread.

Cook's tip: To peel tomatoes, make a small cross using a sharp knife at the base of the tomato. Plunge tomato into simmering water for 30 seconds then into iced water. Remove from water and peel off skin.

Above: Bows with Rich Tomato Basil Sauce, Fresh Tomato Soup
Right: Savoury Mushroom and Ham Crêpes, Sweet Dessert Pancakes

SAVOURY MUSHROOM AND HAM CREPES

Oven temperature 180°C, 350°F, Gas 4

CREPES
- ☐ ¹/₂ cup/60 g/2 oz flour, sifted
- ☐ ³/₄ cup/185 mL/6 fl oz milk
- ☐ 1 egg, lightly beaten
- ☐ 30 g/1 oz butter, melted

MUSHROOM FILLING
- ☐ 1 teaspoon oil
- ☐ ¹/₄ onion, chopped
- ☐ ¹/₄ green pepper, finely sliced
- ☐ 6 button mushrooms, sliced
- ☐ 1 slice ham, chopped
- ☐ freshly ground black pepper
- ☐ 45 g/1¹/₂ oz grated tasty cheese (mature Cheddar)

1 To make filling, heat oil in a nonstick frying pan and cook onion and green pepper over a medium heat for 3-4 minutes or until onion softens. Add mushrooms and ham and cook for 2 minutes longer. Season to taste with black pepper and set aside to cool.

2 To make crêpes, place flour in a bowl and make a well in the centre. Combine milk, egg and butter, pour into well in flour and mix to form a smooth batter. Divide the batter into two portions, cover one and refrigerate. Cook spoonfuls of batter in a lightly greased nonstick frying pan over a medium-high heat for 1-2 minutes each side or until golden. Remove crêpes from pan and set aside to keep warm. Repeat with any remaining batter.

3 Spoon filling down centre of crêpes, sprinkle with half the cheese and roll up. Place crêpes in a small greased ovenproof dish, sprinkle with remaining cheese and cook for 5-8 minutes or until crêpes are heated and cheese melts.

SWEET DESSERT PANCAKES: Add 2¹/₂ tablespoons self-raising flour, ¹/₄ teaspoon baking powder and 1 teaspoon brown sugar to reserved crêpe batter. Whisk to combine. Cook spoonfuls of batter in a lightly greased nonstick frying pan and cook over a medium-high heat for 2-3 minutes each side or until golden. Remove from pan, set aside and keep warm. Repeat with any remaining batter. Serve with a fruit sauce and vanilla ice cream, caramel sauce and whipped cream, sugar and lemon, or chocolate sauce and hazelnut ice cream.

Pikelets or Drop Scones: Use this batter to make pikelets or drop scones for a morning or afternoon tea treat. Add ¹/₂ teaspoon ground cinnamon and 2 tablespoons sultanas to the batter to make spicy fruit pikelets.

Freeze it: You can make the whole batter quantity into crêpes and freeze leftover crêpes between sheets of freezer wrap in a sealed freezer bag. The crêpes can be served for dessert using the same toppings as for Sweet Dessert Pancakes.

ROAST CHICKEN DINNER

Oven temperature 180°C, 350°F, Gas 4

- [ ] **¹/₂ chicken**
- [ ] **1 clove garlic, cut in half**
- [ ] **2 teaspoons fresh rosemary leaves**
- [ ] **1 tablespoon oil**
- [ ] **1 small potato, peeled and halved**
- [ ] **1 piece pumpkin**
- [ ] **1 small carrot, halved**

GRAVY
- [ ] **1 teaspoon flour**
- [ ] **¹/₂ cup/125 mL/4 fl oz chicken stock**
- [ ] **salt and freshly ground black pepper**

1   Wash chicken, then pat dry with absorbent kitchen paper. Rub chicken skin with cut surface of garlic and sprinkle with rosemary. Brush baking dish with oil and place chicken in dish. Arrange vegetables around chicken and bake, basting chicken and vegetables occasionally, for 40 minutes or until chicken and vegetables are cooked. Remove chicken and vegetables from pan. Set aside and keep warm.

2   Place baking dish on the top of stove, stir in flour and cook over a medium heat for 1 minute. Gradually mix in stock and cook, stirring constantly, lifting sediment from base of dish, until mixture boils and thickens. Season to taste with black pepper.

Serving suggestion: Cut chicken in half, set one half aside and serve other half with roast vegetables and gravy.

CHICKEN CASSEROLE: Crush 1 clove garlic, cut ¹/₂ onion into wedges and chop 1 carrot and 1 slice ham. Remove flesh from leftover chicken and set aside. Melt 15 g/¹/₂ oz butter in a saucepan and cook garlic, onion, carrot and ham over a medium heat for 3-4 minutes or until onion softens. Stir in 2 teaspoons flour and cook for 1 minute. Gradually mix in ¹/₂ cup/125 mL/ 4 fl oz chicken stock and 2 teaspoons tomato paste (purée), and cook, stirring constantly, until mixture boils and thickens. Add chicken and 2 teaspoons chopped fresh parsley and simmer for 8 minutes or until carrot is tender. Serve with boiled or steamed rice.

Cook's tip: Leftover chicken should be cooled quickly in the refrigerator to prevent bacteria developing on cooling. Leftover chicken can be made into Chicken Salad with Orange Sauce (page 15).

Below: Roast Chicken Dinner, Chicken Casserole
Right: Spaghetti Bolognese, Cottage Pie

SPAGHETTI BOLOGNESE

Enjoy an authentic Italian meal tonight and tomorrow be comforted with a homely cottage pie.

- ☐ **75 g/2¹/2 oz spaghetti**

BOLOGNESE SAUCE
- ☐ **2 teaspoons olive oil**
- ☐ **1 clove garlic, crushed**
- ☐ **1 small onion, chopped**
- ☐ **1 small carrot, chopped**
- ☐ **1 rasher bacon, chopped**
- ☐ **250 g/8 oz minced lean beef**
- ☐ **3 teaspoons flour**
- ☐ **¹/3 cup/90 mL/3 fl oz red wine**
- ☐ **¹/2 cup/125 ml/4 fl oz beef stock**
- ☐ **1 tablespoon tomato paste (purée)**
- ☐ **¹/2 teaspoon dried oregano**
- ☐ **freshly ground black pepper**

1 Cook spaghetti in boiling water in a saucepan, following packet directions. Drain, set aside and keep warm.

2 To make sauce, heat oil in a nonstick frying pan and cook garlic, onion, carrot and bacon over a medium heat for 3-4 minutes or until onion softens. Add beef and cook for 3-4 minutes longer or until browned.

3 Sprinkle with flour and stir to combine. Gradually mix in wine and stock, stir in tomato paste (purée) and oregano, then reduce heat and simmer for 10 minutes or until sauce thickens. Season to taste with black pepper. Spoon half the sauce over spaghetti.

Serving suggestion: Sprinkle with grated fresh Parmesan cheese.

COTTAGE PIE: To leftover meat sauce add 2 teaspoons tomato sauce, 1 teaspoon of Worcestershire sauce and a dash of Tabasco sauce. Mash 1 small cooked potato with 15 g/¹/2 oz butter and 1 tablespoon milk. Place meat mixture in an individual ovenproof dish and top with mashed potato. Cook in oven at 180°C/350°F/Gas 4 for 15 minutes or until pie is heated.

Cook's tip: Cottage Pie is also delicious made with leftover roast lamb or beef, vegetables, wine, stock and flavourings of your choice. Place all ingredients in a saucepan, bring to simmering and simmer until meat mixture is reduced and thickened. Then place meat mixture in an individual ovenproof dish, top with mashed potato and cook as for Cottage Pie.

Bowl, plate and pie dish The Bay Tree

CAKES AND BISCUITS

Nothing beats the taste of home-baked cakes and biscuits. Many of the goodies in this section keep well. They can also be frozen and they defrost quickly at room temperature.

Chocolate Cake
(recipe page 74)

Plates, cup and saucer Là Maudes

ALMOND FRUIT BREAD

A healthy low-cholesterol treat that keeps well in an airtight container.

Makes 60 slices
Oven temperature 180°C, 350°F, Gas 4

- [ ] **3 egg whites**
- [ ] **1 teaspoon vanilla essence**
- [ ] **$1/2$ cup/100 g/$3^1/2$ oz caster sugar**
- [ ] **1 cup/125 g/4 oz flour, sifted**
- [ ] **155 g/5 oz slivered almonds**
- [ ] **125 g/4 oz glacé cherries, chopped**

1   Place egg whites and vanilla essence in a mixing bowl and beat until soft peaks form. Gradually add sugar, beating well after each addition, until mixture is thick and glossy.

2   Fold in flour, almonds and cherries. Spoon mixture into a greased and lined mini loaf tin. Bake for 35-40 minutes or until cooked when tested with a skewer. Turn onto a wire rack to cool completely.

3   Wrap bread in aluminium foil and set aside for 1-2 days. Using a very sharp serrated knife, cut bread into wafer thin slices. Place slices onto a baking tray lined with baking paper and bake at 150°C/300°F/Gas 2 for 30-35 minutes or until dry and crisp. Cool on a wire rack.

Storage: Almond bread will keep for at least 3 weeks in an airtight container.

CHOCOLATE CAKE

Makes two 20 cm/8 in round cakes
Oven temperature 180°C, 350°F, Gas 4

- [ ] **$3/4$ cup/75 g/$2^1/2$ oz cocoa powder**
- [ ] **$1^1/2$ cups/375 mL/12 fl oz boiling water**
- [ ] **185 g/6 oz butter**
- [ ] **$1^3/4$ cups/390 g/$12^1/2$ oz caster sugar**
- [ ] **2 tablespoons raspberry jam**
- [ ] **3 eggs**
- [ ] **$2^1/4$ cups/315 g/10 oz self-raising flour, sifted**

1   Place cocoa powder and boiling water in a bowl and mix to dissolve. Set aside to cool completely.

2   Place butter, sugar and jam in a mixing bowl and beat until creamy. Beat in eggs one at a time, adding a little flour with each egg. Fold cooled cocoa mixture and remaining flour, alternately, into butter mixture.

3   Spoon mixture into two greased and lined 20 cm/8 in sandwich tins and bake for 35 minutes or until cooked when tested with a skewer. Stand in tins for 5 minutes before turning onto a wire rack to cool completely.

Serving suggestions: Serve cakes sandwiched together with Chocolate Mocha Frosting (see recipe) when entertaining. Cut one cake in half and spread with frosting to have as a treat for morning or afternoon tea. For dessert, accompany cake with hot chocolate sauce and ice cream or cream.

Freeze it: Freeze chocolate cake, iced or uniced, in an airtight freezerproof container or sealed freezer bag. Cut the cakes into halves or even quarters to freeze individually. Just remove the amount you want as you require it and defrost at room temperature for 1-2 hours.

CHOCOLATE MOCHA FROSTING

- [ ] **125 g/4 oz butter**
- [ ] **2 cups/315 g/10 oz icing sugar, sifted**
- [ ] **$1^1/2$ tablespoons cocoa powder, sifted**
- [ ] **2 teaspoons instant coffee powder**
- [ ] **2 tablespoons milk**

Place butter in a small mixing bowl and beat until light and fluffy. Add icing sugar a little at a time, beating well after each addition until creamy. Place cocoa and coffee powders in a small bowl and mix to a smooth paste with milk then beat into butter mixture.

Freeze it: This frosting freezes well in an airtight freezer container. When you want to use the frosting, scoop out amount of frosting required and allow to defrost at room temperature for 30-60 minutes.

Almond Fruit Bread, Chocolate Chip Cookies, Zucchini (Courgette) and Pecan Loaf

CHOCOLATE CHIP COOKIES

Makes 20
Oven temperature 200°C, 400°F, Gas 6

- [ ] **125 g/4 oz butter**
- [ ] **1 cup/170 g/$5^1/2$ oz soft brown sugar**
- [ ] **1 teaspoon vanilla essence**
- [ ] **1 egg**
- [ ] **1 cup/125 g/4 oz flour, sifted**

- ☐ **¹/₂ cup/60 g/2 oz self-raising flour, sifted**
- ☐ **90 g/3 oz desiccated coconut**
- ☐ **125 g/4 oz chocolate chips**

1   Place butter, sugar and vanilla essence in a mixing bowl and beat until creamy. Add egg and beat well.

2   Stir flour, self-raising flour, coconut and chocolate chips into butter mixture. Roll spoonfuls of mixture into balls, place on greased and lined baking trays. Flatten slightly with a spatula and bake for 12-15 minutes. Stand on trays for 2-3 minutes before transferring to a wire rack to cool completely.

Freeze it: These biscuits freeze well in an airtight freezerproof container or sealed freezer bags. Defrost at room temperature for 1-2 hours.

ZUCCHINI (COURGETTE) AND PECAN LOAF

Makes an 11 x 21 cm/4¹/₂ x 8¹/₂ in loaf
Oven temperature 180°C, 350°F, Gas 4

- ☐ **125 g/4 oz butter, softened**
- ☐ **¹/₄ cup/45 g/1¹/₂ oz soft brown sugar**
- ☐ **¹/₄ cup/90 g/3 oz golden syrup**
- ☐ **2 eggs**
- ☐ **3 medium zucchini (courgettes), grated**
- ☐ **75 g/2¹/₂ oz pecans, chopped**
- ☐ **2 cups/250 g/8 oz self-raising flour**
- ☐ **¹/₂ teaspoon ground mixed spice**
- ☐ **¹/₂ teaspoon ground cinnamon**
- ☐ **¹/₂ cup/125 mL/4 fl oz buttermilk or milk**

1   Place butter, sugar and golden syrup in a mixing bowl and beat until light and fluffy. Beat in eggs one at a time, then stir in zucchini (courgettes) and pecans.

2   Sift together flour, mixed spice and cinnamon. Fold flour mixture and buttermilk or milk, alternately, into zucchini mixture. Spoon batter into a greased and lined 11 x 21 cm/4¹/₂ x 8¹/₂ in loaf tin and bake for 40-45 minutes or until cooked when tested with a skewer. Stand in tin for 5 minutes before turning onto a wire rack to cool.

Freeze it: Cut loaf into 4 portions and freeze individually in airtight freezerproof containers or sealed freezer bags. Remove from freezer as required and defrost at room temperature for 1-2 hours. This loaf will defrost more quickly if cut into slices while still frozen.

Tray Home & Garden

PANTRY PLANNER

The following is a guideline to the single cook's well-stocked store cupboard. These are items that are most frequently used and form the basis of many recipes – plus items that add that extra touch.

BASIC ITEMS

- [ ] baking powder
- [ ] bicarbonate of soda
- [ ] breakfast cereal
- [ ] chutneys
- [ ] cocoa powder
- [ ] coconut: desiccated, shredded
- [ ] cornflour
- [ ] dried bread crumbs
- [ ] dried fruits: such as apricots, raisins, sultanas
- [ ] flour: plain, self-raising, whole-meal
- [ ] gelatine
- [ ] golden syrup
- [ ] honey
- [ ] instant coffee
- [ ] jams
- [ ] bottled lemon juice
- [ ] milk: fresh, longlife
- [ ] minced chillies

- minced garlic
- minced ginger
- mustard powder
- selection of nuts: ground, crushed and whole
- selection of pasta
- stock: prepared, powdered or cubes; chicken, beef, vegetable
- oil: vegetable, olive
- relishes
- rice: white, quick-cooking brown
- rolled oats
- sugar: granulated, caster, brown, icing
- tomato paste: individual containers, tubes, or small bottles
- tea
- wine: red, white
- vanilla essence
- vinegar: white, brown, cider

CANNED FOODS

- fruit: such as apricots, peaches, pears
- corn kernels

- peeled tomatoes
- tomato purée
- salmon: small tins
- tuna: small tins

HERBS AND SPICES

- ground black pepper/pepper corns
- chilli powder
- cinnamon: ground, sticks
- curry powder
- dried herbs: such as basil, parsley, oregano, thyme, rosemary, mixed herbs
- ground spices: such as allspice, ginger, nutmeg, mixed spice
- whole cloves

SAUCES AND MUSTARDS

- mayonnaise
- mustards: Dijon, French, wholegrain
- salad dressing
- sauces: such as chilli, cranberry, soy, teriyaki and Worcestershire

PERISHABLE GOODS

- butter or margarine
- cheese: cheddar, Parmesan
- eggs
- milk

BUYING AND STORAGE

- Garlic, ginger and chillies are all sold in minced (ground) form in bottles ready to use. They are an economical alternative to the fresh item and ideal for the single cook's kitchen.
- Prepared stock is also available as a long-life product or fresh from some butchers.
- Fresh pasta cooks in less time than dried. It can be stored in the freezer, and so makes a sensible alternative to dried pasta.
- Store dry ingredients in well-labelled airtight containers
- Store onions and root vegetables such as potatoes and turnips in a cool, dark, dry place.
- Store meat, poultry and fish on a plate covered with plastic food wrap in the refrigerator.

Index